# ON THE
# ART
# OF THE
# CRAFT

Quote on p. 39  Sartre, Jean-Paul, and Lloyd Alexander. "Section 1." Essay. In Nausea, 8–8. New York, N.Y.: New Direction, 2007.

Quote on p. 39  Dickens, Charles. A Tale of Two Cities, 2016. https://www.gutenberg.org/files/98/old/2city12p.pdf.

For information, write to:
Girls Write Now, Inc. 247 West 37th Street, Suite 1000
New York, NY 10018
info@girlswritenow.org
girlswritenow.org

FIRST EDITION

Library of Congress Cataloging-in-Publication Data has been applied for.

ISBN 978-0-06-341770-0

24 25 26 27 28  LBC  5 4 3 2 1

# ON THE
# ART
# OF THE
# CRAFT

## A GUIDEBOOK TO COLLABORATIVE STORYTELLING

# A Note from the Girls Write Now Editorial Advisory Committee

TWENTY-FIVE YEARS AGO, Girls Write Now began as a grassroots organization centered on two ideas: that storytelling is powerful, and that there needs to be more space for women writers to tell their stories. Today, Girls Write Now is one of the top organizations for creative youth mentorship, cultivating a powerhouse of voices leading us all into the future. With mentees and mentors in over 36 states, a robust curriculum of programming, and a strong, inspired community of writers, we are proving that storytelling not only serves to capture our world as it is, but to shape the one we hope to see. Storytelling allows us to learn from the past, reckon with the present, and imagine new futures. As storytellers, we appear to pluck entire worlds out of thin air and bring them into existence. It is, in many ways, an act of magic.

The definition of *alchemy* describes it as a process of creation, combination, and transformation—a way to make something new out of what exists. Storytelling might seem an act of magic, but in truth it is a process of continual collaboration, inspiration, and hard work. It is also one where voices have historically been silenced, leaving that magic for only a handful to possess.

The stories in this collection reclaim that magic, pulling histories out from oppressive silence and disrupting conventional norms in the writing field. Through collaboration, these writers and their mentors create new worlds, combine knowledge, and transform their readers. They merge time, breaking down binaries and blurring borders to imagine new futures. They weave together alternate experiences to find common ground. They challenge us to try on truth and see the world around us from a different perspective, showing us what is beautiful. They demonstrate the craft of writing.

Creativity is not some magic, inaccessible thing. There is an artist in all of us that needs to be nurtured. At Girls Write Now, our work is to uncover each and every storyteller's individual magic through the power of community. We are not only a community of exceptional people, but are made exceptional *through* community.

When we began thinking about a book that could speak to Girls Write Now's twenty-five year history, we knew we wanted to demonstrate how we were creating, combining, and transforming the literary landscape through mentoring the next generation of writers, whose voices come together here across past, present, and future.

This book was shaped over the last year by Girls Write Now's Editorial Advisory Committee, made up of current mentees, program alumni, and publishing professionals lending their wisdom. Together, the group decided the themes and structure for the book, supported the editorial process, and participated in a variety of forums reimagining how we view storytelling in today's world. This book demonstrates a groundbreaking collaborative approach to the creative process, each voice building on the next to contribute to the whole.

# GIRLS WRITE NOW EDITORIAL ADVISORY COMMITTEE

### COMMITTEE CHAIR

Spencer George

### COMMITTEE CO-CHAIRS

Emily Mendelson
Richelle Szypulski

### COMMITTEE MEMBERS

Julia Andresakis
Nana Ekua Brew-Hammond
Maya Cruz
Kathryn Destin
Denise Domena
Morayo Faleyimu
Kaya Fraser
Liliana Hopkins
Kat Jagai
Vahni Kurra
Giftbelle Lomotey
Erica Silberman
Joy L. Smith
Abby West
Monika Woods
Lauren Young
Rachel Young

Current mentees were challenged here to select a piece written by a mentee over the last twenty-five years and respond to, continue, or adapt it into a piece of their own. In addition, mentees developed prompts out of the pieces they wrote, inviting new writers to continue the conversation.

We invite you to step into the worlds crafted here— between wooded forests and crowded sidewalks, beyond limits and before the mirror, amongst towering mountains and high school classrooms—and allow them to transform you.

## Tell Your Story

Submit your responses to these prompts to Girls Write Now Stories for a chance to be published on our site.

# CONTENTS

*Note: Stories that depict sensitive topics are necessary for many reasons. Shedding light on the most challenging parts of the human experience can both help others feel less alone and inspire readers to work toward a better future. However, we recognize that certain topics may be distressing when they catch readers off guard. That is why we have included a Content Warning for some of the stories.*

## Creation

# Combination

# Transformation

# Incantation

# About Girls Write Now

# CREATION

*So often we're waiting for inspiration to hit us, to just pop up like the tooth fairy. It'll fly in your room like a little bug and leave a story right under your pillow and now you have somewhere to begin. But when you're a student of the craft and you're always playing with this beautiful art form of story, inspiration means finding that peculiar beauty in just about everything, in the everyday functions of life. A pillow can become poetic. Who are we to say that it isn't?*

— JASMINE MANS, Girls Write Now
Teaching Artist, Poet, and Author of
*Black Girl, Call Home*

# A Slight Misunderstanding

by JOY L. SMITH, 2011

*An exploration of self and how the world sees you.*

I wasn't doing anything out of the ordinary. I was just being Joy, being ten at a restaurant and heading to the bathroom. Normally my twin sister, Cherish, would have gone with me because we were always told "go with your sister," but for some reason I went alone.

I dressed how I felt comfortable, in what was my favorite thing at the time. Some girls wore jewelry or tutus. I was in love with my Sprewell jersey and Lee jeans. They were loose and fit with what the boys were wearing. I was a baller, and to complete my outfit I topped it off with my fitted hat that covered my zigzag braids and headed for the bathroom.

What was I thinking? Nothing. It was a bathroom; of course other women would be in there. It was no big deal. Despite my attire, I was a girl, and I had full access. As soon as I stepped one foot in the bathroom a lady held her wet hands out as if to stop me and said, "Papi, you're in the wrong bathroom!"

"Huh?" I said.

Suddenly, I was confused and angry and of course embarrassed because, well, people were now looking at me. I was naïve, I realize now. I was at that age where boys and girls were at the same height and my secondary characteristics hadn't developed yet, so it was easy to mistake me as a boy.

Still, a boy was the last thing I was. I didn't think I looked like a boy; besides, I had two earrings in my ear. Duh, boys don't wear two earrings, I thought to myself. As I sat back at the table upset and slightly embarrassed, I whined to my godmother that the lady thought I was a boy and Spanish. She told me it was just a mistake, but I was furious. This lady needed her eyes checked. But then Cherish said, "You did it to yourself, Joy. Stop dressing like a boy and no one will think you're a boy. You're not a boy, Joy," she said angrily at me.

I wasn't the one she should be angry at. I was glaring at her. I wanted to burn a hole in her face. The lady already hurt my feelings; I didn't need her hurting mine, too. Didn't anyone get that my feelings were bruised? This was a serious situation for me, and no one was getting it or trying to make it better. And my own twin at that! She should be on my side. But this was a common statement with her. She always had something to say about my clothing. "Are you really going to wear that jersey again?" or, "Take that hat off."

From then on, I slowly stopped wearing my baller hoodies, fitted hats, and my prized jersey. I would never be mistaken again. Before my transformation was complete, I was playing basketball with a group of boys, killing them of course, when a boy asked:

"Are you a boy or a girl?"

I swooshed a three before telling him, "I'm a girl." I was never mistaken again.

---

*Joy L. Smith is a former mentee from '09-'11. She is an early childhood teacher, huge theater nerd and author of* Turning, *a YA contemporary novel.*

# A Foreshadowed Understanding
### by AREN LAU, 2023

*People often struggle with their genders growing up. Most grow out—
or, rather—into their pre-established identities. I didn't.*

I could never seem to break the formula. What was it about me that confused people? Was it something in my eyes? My voice? My arms? I'm five-foot-three—it couldn't be my height. For a while, I had long hair, too. So what was going on? Why couldn't people understand that I was trying so hard, wishing so incessantly that they see I was a girl?

My mirror didn't seem to agree with me either. *Boy*, it told me. *Boy in a dress.* This didn't make sense to me . . . so it had to be wrong. Everyone else must have felt this way, too, right? At any rate, until I was fifteen, I was determined to pride myself on my "womanhood," take on this label and do with it what I could. But at the same time . . .

"Is that your older brother?" people would ask my younger sibling, every time I was within his friends' line of vision. And I would shrink inside myself with embarrassment because I knew if I just looked at my reflection, I would see that these little kids were not unreasonable.

"Are you a boy or a girl?" asked a toddler I was babysitting, with a glimmer of innocent curiosity in her eyes. At that point, as a fourteen-year-old, I didn't know how to answer her question. All I said was, "Some people…" and then trailed off, much to the child's disappointment. Then as I watched her bottom lip start to tremble the way kids' mouths often do, I felt a spark of hatred burst faintly inside myself, because I couldn't be the role model I knew this little girl wanted.

"Why do you dress like a boy?"

It's more comfortable.

"Why did you cut your hair?"

It's easier.

"Why don't you like it when people call you pretty?"

It's weird.

"Sorry, excuse me, sir."

Oh, no, I'm… never mind.

Every time Easter rolled around, I had to step into a dress my mother had so kindly picked out for me. Don't get me wrong—I was grateful. However, I felt like the outfit—though not necessarily tight—was strangling me. The wind was too breezy between my legs, the neckline felt too low, the flattering sandals were scratchy on my feet. I wanted to throw a blanket over myself and hide in the dark forever, but I was forced to go to church anyway, where people would eye me with confusion ... Why, why, why? What *was* it about me that made people hesitate before they spoke? And why did I feel the exact same way?

My mother scolded me for my eventual hatred of my sex, the implicit misogyny in such a notion ... That wasn't really what I was getting at, though. I didn't hate women. I hated myself.

By my sophomore year, I had learned a little about the nuances of gender through the Internet, and saw an opportunity, a spot for myself. I decided that my pronouns would be *they/them*. At once, the burden of femininity was lifted off my shoulders, and I felt that I could breathe deeply for the first time in my life. Even so, I cried as I watched it go. There was nothing wrong with being a woman ... but there was something wrong with *me* being a woman. That was for sure. Unfortunately, this non-binary euphoria didn't last long, either. Once I had stepped into the wild, I could feel that there was a stronger truth awaiting me, something *right*, but certainly more extreme.

Now, as is often the case with situations like these, I feel like the world has reversed. Even though I've fully socially transitioned into the more comfortable mold of *boy*, all I get is "She, she, she." The universe is unfair, but what can you do? I know the feeling of walking into a bathroom—either one—and getting stares of both puzzlement and even hostility. I know that feeling deep within me. It's complicated, it's frustrating, and it seems unfixable.

Despite this, the only thing I can do is be *me*. However people see me, I know who and what I am, and nobody's ignorant opinion or snide comment will ever sway me ... if they only knew how much I've hit myself with those same arguments. Trust me, it doesn't work. I recently wore my first tux to Senior Picture Day, and a suit to church on Easter, much to my family's astonishment and my own strange relief. A few months ago, someone came up to me during art class and asked, "Are you a boy or a girl?"

This time, I was able to put aside my doubts, and answer easily: "I'm a boy."

Then I went back to minding my own business.

---

*Aren Lau, an eighteen-year-old half-Hongkongese novelist, actually hates writing a lot, but for some reason just keeps doing it because he is insane. He lives in Brooklyn.*

**Tell Your Story**

**A Prompt from Aren Lau**

Write about something you hate about yourself, and then reflect on why there's also a lot to love about it.

# Space
## by TAMMY CHAN, 2011

*Growing up is tough. We miss nap times we didn't want to take, the easy home-work we didn't want to do. Thinking back to the good life as a college student.*

*Kid*

"When are you going to throw away all those science boards? They're taking up space!" my mom would ask me every time she took out the garbage. I never could quite answer her because a part of me didn't ever want to let them go. It was a collection of four boards, each decorated with construction paper and glitter. They were three years' worth of my brilliantly-and-geniusly-put-together science projects.

Third grade: *Float or Sink.* "Oh, this pencil case is definitely gonna sink!" I said. "Yeah right, I bet it floats!" my partner, Kayla said. It sank. I was pretty genius, I'd say.

Fourth grade: *Which Bean Grows the Fastest.* The Lima bean, of course! I was right. Like I said: genius.

Fifth grade: *Do Plants Grow More in the Dark or the Light.* Light, of course! Need I say? Genius.

I was proud of my projects, always boasting about them when I'd have to carry the large tri- board to school the morning of the science fair. It was HUGE, much bigger than my small stature could handle while walking the three long blocks to school. My mom walked beside me, holding my book bag so that I could be a big girl for those few minutes, lugging the board to school all by myself. By the time I'd get to school, there'd be creases near the bottom two corners from the poster dragging along the ground as I walked. But what really mattered—the colors, the glitter, the fact that my guess had been proven—was intact. Bringing them home was just as bad, but what choice did I have? I couldn't just let the teacher throw them away—not after all that effort.

*Now*

I should have thrown the science boards away at school, like all the other kids. I'd watch them after the science fair, laughing as they demolished their projects by kicking them, throwing them, and sliding on them across the gymnasium floor. But not me. Three years I did it. Three years in a row I stayed up late decorating the board, adding those last touches of glitter and drawing the final squiggly lines.

Third grade: The classic float-or-sink experiment (or, to sound fancy, "measuring an object's buoyancy"), in which we threw random objects into a tub filled with water and ended up having a mini-water fight in the bathroom.

Fourth grade: Which bean grows the fastest, employing the bootleg method of growing them in a Ziploc bag with a square of paper towel and staples to support the beans' roots?

Fifth grade: Do plants grow more in the dark or light? Are you kidding me?

The three classics of science-fair experiments, the ones every kid in the school did. Did they measure my intelligence? Not at all.

I would kill to have projects like those again for school. In high school, there's no more need for crayons, colored pencils, markers, construction paper—and especially not glitter. I miss those days when the hardest assignment I had was a science-fair project. Now it's just papers—black print on a white background. BORING! I used to have time, time to kill—staying up until, at the latest, NINE O'CLOCK! I even daringly stayed up to 9:30 p.m. once, JUST once, because I ran out of glue and had to rummage all over the house to find something sticky.

Nothing could have stopped me before, but now—everything could. Time. Work. School. College. Parents. Boyfriend. Friends. Hunger. Coldness. Hotness. Crazy weather. Snow after 70-degree warmth. Nothing to watch on TV. Tiredness. iPhone dying. Forgot my headphones. Annoying buskers on the train—the untalented ones. Wrong-number calls. Wrong-number calls at 4:30 in the morning. No gum in my bag. Broken nail. Bad hair days. Hair not cooperating. No more money on my MetroCard. Spending a big chunk of my paycheck on a new MetroCard. Unnecessary random bag frisks in the train station during the morning rush hour AND afternoon rush hour. Fat policemen in their cars blocking the bus stop. No buses in the morning. The twenty-minute walk to the train. Crowded trains. Morning commutes. Tourists. Crappy coffee. Drama. Drama. Drama. Drama queens. Drama kings. Just drama.

Some days it's hard to tell if I'll sink or float.

---

*Tammy Chan is a local TV news producer in Los Angeles. She graduated with a Broadcast Journalism degree from Syracuse University. She was born and raised in New York City.*

# Time
## by JILLIAN DANESHWAR, 2023

*Time. A constant which creates change. Change in relationships, personalities, and perspectives are explored in this piece.*

**11:05 a.m.**

Nap time. My head lowered, but never my eyelids. I could never shake my raging mind. Quiet plagued my poor little frame. Such a shame, I learned to lie at such a young age.

**12:22 p.m.**

Safety scissors and glue. Clueless kids and cyclical lessons. My attention drifted out the window, watching cars and falling snow.

**12:49 p.m.**

I couldn't be bothered to group little lines. Fervently, I'd multiply and divide in my mind. I'd turn in my paper before time. I'm sent to aid the students who misbehaved.

**1:47 p.m.**

Finally, a science lesson. What do trees breathe? $CO_2$. I learned that if you answer too much, the teacher stops calling on you.

**2:12 p.m.**

Dismissal. No more work for the rest of the day. I'd have the rest of the afternoon to play.

**8:00 a.m.**

Repeat.

A decade slips by.

No sleeping in class. I beg my consciousness not to crash. Past lies become the truth. My eyelids droop.

My mind still shifts; it's hard to control. X and V, I can't escape cut and paste. Different windows occupy my attention. Clueless kids, we have a faster connection.

The bell rang, and I took my test. I did my best, but it's the grade that matters. A fact hammered in my head over eleven grades, its importance growing everyday.

Classes end, yet I stay. Work until five. Get home. Work until nine. That's a lie. Work until midnight. Get a wink of sleep. What a wonderful day.

Repeat.

---

*Jillian Daneshwar is a junior in high school who has a passion for and dedication to writing and robotics. She has accumulated numerous awards in both fields.*

## Tell Your Story

### A Prompt from Jillian Daneshwar

You can send one Post-it note back to your 10-year-old self. What would you say?

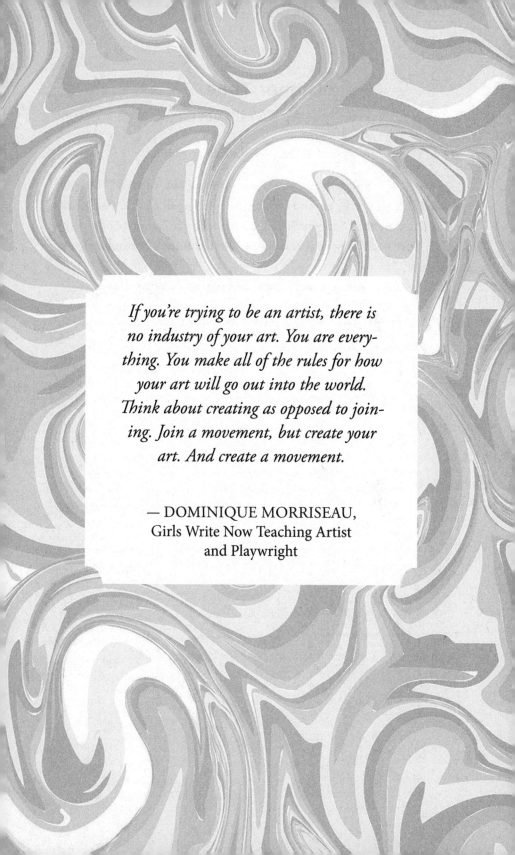

*If you're trying to be an artist, there is no industry of your art. You are everything. You make all of the rules for how your art will go out into the world. Think about creating as opposed to joining. Join a movement, but create your art. And create a movement.*

— DOMINIQUE MORRISEAU,
Girls Write Now Teaching Artist
and Playwright

# Dinner Time

## by JOANNE LIN, 2011

*The dynamics of dinner as a Chinese family.*

The summer air wraps tight against the room. "How was your day?" Ma asks. Her voice drifts into the air and collides with the smell of rice. Chopsticks bang into one another. Soft words said as a battle for the last piece of broccoli emerges. Taste buds, they sway and dance. Stomachs dissolve into happiness, smiles erupt.

This love, rare as it is, stumbles and falls into an everyday routine.

---

*Joanne Lin (she/her) is a Girls Write Now mentee alum residing in Brooklyn.*

# Subtle, But Soft

## by MEGUMI JINDO, 2023

*Inspired by Joanne Lin's 2011 writing and fueled by the passion of
my mother's love, this piece was penned with fervor and a learning
heart of the beauty in subtleties.*

As I finish brushing my teeth and prepare to go to sleep, I step into the dimly lit granite kitchen and reach for a hug from my mom. A usual routine, and yet somehow, when the side of her face rests against the top of my head, and my face is pressed against her beige-colored apron, and her hands—skin peeling from the numerous times she has washed her children's plates, the love she has spent for us—wrap around me: it's then. It's when her voice softly, with vivid warmth, murmurs, "Goodnight—sleep well and stay healthy, okay?" that I feel the most comfort. The rarest glance of love, but a love that shines the brightest.

But then, there are times like these, on a gloomy October Friday. "Mom, why can't I go to my friend's sweet 16th birthday party?" I exasperatedly sigh, having been arguing for the past ten minutes.

"I told you why. We are not talking about this again. You were sick just this Monday, and especially because of last year's hospital incident, you can't go. This whole week you have been busy with no time to rest."

Mom keeps mixing the fresh green snap peas with the sautéed onions. I lean against the fridge, crossing my arms with a frown, staring at my brothers who are playing chess across the kitchen, and retort, "But I took a nap like yesterday, and I'm okay now—I want to go. You never let me go to the things that I want, so let me at least go to this one." Mom doesn't look up at me as my voice cracks at the end of the sentence, continuing to stir the vegetables. She opens the cabinets to her left, pulls out a navy blue salt shaker, and sprinkles salt over them.

"I know you want to go, but your health is not the best right now—"

"It's better now, though." I turn around to look at her angry face and continue, "And all my friends will be there and it's not even that far."

Mom's face, as I stare at her, is tired, proof that rising from bed in the early mornings to prepare for our school days takes a toll on her. "No, you cannot go because you do not do your own responsibilities and your body is exhausted. You don't even have enough time to rest on the weekends, anyway—"

"Mom—"

"No. End of discussion. You will not go. It's unfortunate that you can't go but if you go to this party, this weekend, you will end up in the ER again, and your health will then get to the point where it won't even mend on its own. So, no." She looks up at me, once, as she transfers the cut mushrooms into the already sizzling pan, and ignores my glaring looks. I stalk away from the kitchen, tears bubbling, with the sound of her chopping echoing in the tension-filled silence.

But it's the times on other nights like the ones when I kick off the covers at night—in the stuffy room, unconsciously opening the window, letting in the starry sky's breeze—and mom comes in to check on me, repositioning the indigo comforters and closing the window so I don't wake up shivering, that I'm reminded of how much I'm loved by the very mother I sometimes think doesn't understand me.

When she holds my hand as tears stream down my pale face in the hospital room, as some sort of medicine takes hold of me, which makes my vision turn the doctor's hand from one to two to three. Calling out "Mom, Mom" in Japanese, for no reason, alarming my poor mother, she comes hovering over me, hugging me. Desperately trying to figure out what is wrong—asking the nurses and doctors why I am like this, why I am acting this way—did they put too much of a numb spray for the PICC line placement in the ICU? It's here, then, now that I'm overwhelmingly reminded of how much love can save a person, and how much a parent loves a child—how much a mother loves her daughter. How much her soft voice is my soothing resolution, how much her nurturing crinkled hands hold, how much her ripening body loves a child who never takes the time to appreciate her enough. It's always enough. The little rare moments of love disguised as an everyday brush-away routine—it's there, even if it may not seem as appealing as all the other mothers who buy ice cream on a sweltering day for their child, hold hands while walking home, or give a supportive cheer for their children's sport's games, school colors smeared on their cheeks. The love for me is there.

It's here, then, now, and will always be—the proof of the strength of the love between a daughter and her mother.

*Megumi Jindo is a junior in high school in New York City. She's a huge overuser of em dashes and loves reading, music, and poetry.*

## Tell Your Story

### A Prompt from Megumi Jindo

Write a poem reflecting on what limits your own love may have at times, whether familial, friendly, or romantic.

# Requiem
## by ANTONIA BRUNO, 2007

*This piece is the story of my family coping with my aunt's
cancer diagnosis and the role of music in bringing
people together and getting through hard times.*

On the last Christmas that my aunt was alive we played music. We always play music, but this time we played with a new level of ferocity and passion. My father hit every piano key as though it was the only sound worth creating in the world, and cousin Will beat his hands on the bongos as though he were sacrificing his fingers for his mother's life. Even my uncle who was tone deaf and preferred to listen had joined in, and the younger cousins whacked tambourines off beat. We had been playing for hours, and our faces were red.

It was a cold December day, but we were sweating through our T-shirts.

She sat on the couch between her mother and sister, thin and white as a sheet of paper. Her cheeks were hallowed out as though they'd been punched in and got stuck that way. She had a scarf wrapped around her bald head, but it was coming undone and it took too much strength for her to reach up and fix it so the loose ends hung down her back. She had given up wigs a few months before. Wigs were for pretending that everything was okay, and we couldn't pretend anymore. One too many discussions about the future without Aunt Heidi had stripped us of the illusions created by smiles and wigs. We had been pushed to honesty. Forced to have raw and heart-breaking conversations we never imagined having, ones that left us stumbling shell shocked on the sidewalk outside her house. Ones that left us bolting upright every time the phone rang, our hearts stopping for a second before we answered. But it was Christmas and she was still with us, her closeness to death somehow bringing new energy into the warm room. Energy that infiltrated our music, bringing notes to life and making melodies into dedications.

We played songs from her 1960s childhood, songs of resistance and revolution. We played songs from my childhood, ones that my father had sung to me as I was falling asleep so they wove into my dreams and wrote themselves on the inside of my mind. Familiar lyrics took on a new quality on this day, seeming to be filled with messages I had never heard before and simple chords that struck me as unimaginably beautiful. I thought of the way these songs comforted me, the way the gentle guitar accompaniment made me feel safe, and I wondered if after this day they would make me sad.

My aunt sat on the couch and listened, her head tipped back slightly, and we knew that if she were strong enough she would have been smiling. She seemed to know that the music was for her, that we were playing her favorite songs because we were saying goodbye. Once she started singing along, so softly it was almost a whisper. We heard it as though it was the only sound in the room. As though she were screaming in our ears.

My other aunt stood next to me, and tears ran silently down her cheeks as she sang. Tears that we had kept hidden at past family gatherings. Tears that we held back until we left the room, went for a walk, locked ourselves in the bathroom during Thanksgiving dinner and flushed the toilet to muffle our sobs. Tears that came when we watched movies about death, and made us feel ashamed because we didn't want to act like she was already dead.

Those were the wig days. Now they were tears we no longer bothered to hide, because we all knew in our hearts it was the last time.

So, we just kept playing.

As though if we strummed a little harder she would live a little longer. As though if we sang a little louder, she could fight a little harder. As though when we stopped, she, too, would stop, and we couldn't let that happen. Or maybe we just didn't know what else to do. Maybe we had realized that we couldn't save her, that cancer had somehow beat love. So, we turned to music and hoped that it would be stronger than us. We sang songs from her childhood, songs of resistance and revolution. Music has always been our resistance. We find notes to say "goodbye." Notes to say, "I love you more than I have words to express." Notes to say, "it's okay. You can go. We won't stop playing when you're gone."

---

*Antonia Bruno is a Girls Write Now mentee alum and current mentor. She is a public defender and co-author of the children's book series* Josie Goes Green.

# Melodic Grief:
# A Tragic Manifestation

by SALMA ELHANDAOUI, 2023

*CW: mentions of death and violence.*

*Grief, love, and family are three concepts of immense power, but they can be unexplainable in their collective form. For an individual to eradicate any grief that has swallowed their soul is quite impossible.*

Yesterday was October 29th, 2022, a day of horror and unimaginable pain. It was a nightmare of this generation and a day that will never be forgotten. It's a day that will stick with me for eternity. Seeing people compressed together with no space to walk, no space to breathe, no space to talk, but only a space to scream. There is only space to scream your lungs out for help, for home, for hope that you will be saved, that you will be one of the few people to escape this tragedy. The Itaewon Halloween crowd surge involved over 100,000 people gathering for a Halloween party after two years of gathering restrictions; over 100 people died and many others were injured from the incident. As people were performing CPR on victims, Western music was playing loudly in the background with many noises running through the dark alleys. What was more horrifying to imagine were parents picking up their phones in the morning, only to hear that their child had passed away or was severely injured.

Grief, love, and family are three concepts of immense power. When I imagine grieving over a family member's death, I can only feel tingling bloodshed running through my soul. This is when music comes to rescue me from the discomfort caused by unfortunate events. When I think about tragic situations like the Itaewon Halloween Tragedy, "Eight," a song by IU, a South Korean musical artist, soothes my distressed mind. It reminds me that you can't anticipate when your loved one will be gone from the world. You never know when your loved one would leave you all alone without a goodbye to establish some sort of closure. To believe that your loved one is indeed fine and will come back after a fun party ends. To believe that your loved one will stay with you for many years to come. To believe your loved one will always be there for you as long as you live. To only hear that they will never be by your side again. Only to hear that they're dead and gone from this world.

When listening to music about grief and mourning, you can feel the memories run through a lane of sadness. But music has a sort of incredible universality that can wave your heart like smooth liquid as it journeys you to the past that you desperately want back, to the past you would never let go of if given the chance. You might need some soothing or sad music to console your mind, your body, your heart, and your life. It might ease your depression, your anxiety, and your frustration. It might remind you of that amazing loved one who you will never forget, not in a million years. Music has the power to shift your soul to heaven and put a smile on your face or comfort you during difficult times. The feeling of losing someone you loved or someone related to you can be the most heartbreaking emotion in your lifetime. Losing someone who read you books at night, cooked dinner for you every day, listened to your concerns, or gave you meaningful advice could break your heart right through the middle as if it's slicing all the love you had left.

Imagine sitting down on your couch one day watching your favorite TV show and laughing by yourself. You imagine living a normal life with your loved ones, with your tribe, and with your people. You imagine all these people fading away in the blink of an eye. But you eventually hear a lonely yet beautiful voice pour out of your soul. You join this voice and together you journey to a valley that echoes with many voices, giving you a glittering hope for the future. This is how music tells you that you're not alone in this world.

---

*Salma Elhandaoui is a creative writer, photographer, and contemporary literature analyst. She is a high school senior and has written articles on scientific topics and neurological disorders for the* Murrow Network, *her school's award-winning newspaper.*

## Tell Your Story

### A Prompt from Salma Elhandaoui

How does your family express grief and honor loved ones who have passed away? What cultural traditions or religious ideologies shape your family's expression of mourning?

# Tell Your Story
## A Prompt from Arisa White

Bring attention to someone whose absence has affected
you. Where do you feel it in your body?

Bring your hands to that part of your body. Breathe
into it and exhale making a hum. Write down the part
of your body. Describe the feeling as a series of colors
and objects.

Ask your absence a question. Write this question down.

---

*Arisa White is a Cave Canem fellow, Sarah Lawrence College alumna,
MFA graduate from the University of Massachusetts, Amherst, and author
of the poetry chapbooks* Disposition for Shininess, Post Pardon, Black
Pearl, Perfect on Accident, *and* "Fish Walking" & Other Bedtime
Stories for My Wife *won the inaugural Per Diem Poetry Prize.*

# THE 17 MOONS
## by WILLOW ROSADO, 2022

*The love letter is written.*

Write a love letter
Meet the standards
Express the love of this thing, place, item, person
Go in-depth of these emotions
A love letter
Must not lack these emotions
But sometimes can cause a commotion
In your mind
My love letter
Must be taken and flown with the wind
We must read it across the deepest length of the oceans
It must be sung to the swaying of the trees
It must run through the wind blowing the love away
The animals must imagine it so they can connect to it all day
Although I shouldn't forget the people
It must be described with imagery to the people so they can feel emotions
from far away
And
Visualize
But to the moon, it must be written
Written well
Because it shines, providing, it's listening to the poems, to the breaths, to the
cries for help
It's there
Staring down

We haven't met, but I often see you
I take pictures to remember what phase I discovered you in
From new, waxing crescent, first quarter, waxing gibbous, full moon, waning
gibbous, third quarter, waning crescent

There's never an exact feeling I can delineate you as
You make the goose-bumps along my skin rise
You make my cheeks turn red with all my acne, scars, and oily skin
My body turns cold becoming paralyzed at the moment, as the sweat drips
off my palms
My fingers tremble all at once
All causing a stop in my pulse
This brings me to a high degree
Pulling you closer
A moment you build awareness, finding truth
A door you open
Built with my imagination, turning different colors, with different textures, shapes
My eyes flash with lights
Ready to explore
Knowing I felt like this before
I always feel this connection within my soul, spirit, emotional being, physical
being
You don't see me from the close but you know me from the far
You influence a character in me
Within me, to me, and through me
You hold my eyes with all your light
Capturing me in a moment
I neither run nor hide from these feelings but build a sense within
We are mature lovers
Deeply in love
Showing, sharing, expressing it every time
There is no doubt that we are beyond the years of ink I press on paper writing
a love letter to you
Our love is timeless
But all needs to end
As my planet ends
Your planet is never-ending, your start is your end, your end is your begin-
ning
We are a chemical reaction
Burning others around
The moon eclipsed

The human heart feels you
Surrounding yourself with more stars
You are my light
The stars around me
My sight of freedom
You are the moon
In a crescent

The love letter is written

---

*Willow Rosado is a writer from Brooklyn. Some of their interests include drawing, spiritual practices, cooking, and cleaning. In their free time, Willow is focused on creating an upcoming podcast and writing poetry.*

# Time is a Strange Mother
### by ZIYING JIAN, 2023

*A love letter—inspired by Ocean Vuong's* Time is a Mother—*to the moments that shape us, reminding us to cherish each one as it comes and goes. Each piece reflects on the beauty and pain of existing within the intricacies of time.*

we're making out on your bed. the clatter of our teeth underscores our naïveté to this new love. my thoughts fly back to a few months ago to your sofa where i sat with my arms wrapped around you, my face crushed into your neck because i was scared of what kissing you on the lips would mean. i shouldn't have been so fearful. soft breaths fill your room, moving day to slumber, and finally to lasting darkness. we're losing ourselves before time seeks to tear us apart, and warp our skin with a million cuts of nostalgia. i learned to make paper hearts to soften the cuts. in fact, you have one on the back of your phone made of a green gum wrapper. it rests on top of a polaroid picture of me, and i rest easy knowing time stops somewhere—on the surface of a photograph and the lifted corners of your lips, suspended in charm.

❋ ❋ ❋ ❋ ❋ ❋ ❋

I am chasing the setting sun. Left and right, left and right. I lean into the forces underneath my feet and sway to the rhythm of my wheels. I ride over the potholes, sewer grates, and bumps. Cars flank me from either side and lay a path for me to run and glide and fly. I'm rollerblading down the block in the afternoon, and it feels like time will never reach me. Perhaps I'll kick powerfully enough to float into the white cotton scattered above. But then dusk moves into night. My thoughts quiet down and I come to a stop.

the moon pierces through the clouds
there is no time to bask in its cold glow
time is like a strange mother
calling me home

❋ ❋ ❋ ❋ ❋ ❋ ❋

My room faces the direction where birds fly from. Around this time of the year, I wake up plunged into what feels like an ice bath. I turn on my space heater and wiggle my toes. These days, I pay no mind to the tangled knots in my hair and my dried lips. I browse through the various titles in my

Kindle library. Dickens's *A Tale of Two Cities*, Ocean Vuong's *On Earth We're Briefly Gorgeous*, and Sartre's *Nausea* among others. It is a delineating choice that I'm excited to sink my teeth into. Rare.

As the words spread out and warmth washes over me, my day becomes measued not by the hours of a clock, but, instead, by the participation of my heart.

how every fiber of my chest is wrung
twisted
stretched
mercilessly attacked
and then filled
soothed
reassured
by these voices on the page
"I am alone in the midst of these happy, reasonable voices"
sartre writes to me

I read, and I read, and I continue to read until the sky changes from a soft blue into a fiery red. I eat Lucky Charms and Goldfish crackers in bed. I even find the courage to start working on a new coding project, but I still avoid GitHub. There is comfort imbued into these words, and I feel a little less dread. I do not even waste a moment to ponder where else I could be until—

—I wake up.

＊＊＊＊＊＊＊＊

...

＊＊＊＊＊＊＊＊

There is a white ceiling above me. I groan and try to go back to sleep. But it's too late. Time is a strange mother. She wakes and charges forward with the day. I submit to her whims because, in reality, I know nothing else.

In my dream, I'm twirling my hair while flipping through Charles Dickens' *A Tale of Two Cities*. "You have been the last dream of my soul. A dream, all a dream that ends in nothing," proclaims Sydney Carton as he confesses his love to Lucie Manette. Even in my dream, that line unsettles me.

I tell myself I have dreams, but it is perhaps a losing battle to lie to yourself. Dreams are a destination's end and I don't ever want to end. Periods are where I begin. Time is where I continue to exist. In fact, this is my love letter to wasted time. I write to you because I want you to know that you are not wasted. I am a creature exploring your time, delicately at times and with difficulty most of the time. You are like a surprise when you remove yourself without permission. But regardless, you are everything to me.

✳ ✳ ✳ ✳ ✳ ✳ ✳

*you tell me that when you snap your fingers, you hope i appear. i am not magic, but perhaps we are magical in our own way. we're waltzing on your kitchen floor as you teach me how to ballroom dance. my feet get stuck on your ankles, a laugh erupts, and the occasional cat crawls around. i stumble sometimes, but you hold onto me firmly despite it all. with our hands clasped together, we sway and float and glide in all directions. time doesn't stop for anyone, not even for us. but we've learned to bend it in wonderful ways. that is our magic.*

---

*Ziying Jian (ZEE-ying, she/her) is a high school senior who's passionate about investigating storytelling in all mediums. Immigrating from China at age five, she now coordinates her school's theater community and writes stories on her Notes app.*

## Tell Your Story

### A Prompt from Ziying Jian

Recall a moment where you've lost track of time. Write about why the experience was rewarding or memorable.

# I'm Finally Home

## by MEDELIN CUEVAS, 2016

*This piece is a nostalgic and intimate moment in my life reliving the origin of my familiar roots and giving me a sense of belonging in my native country.*

I remember the smell of palm trees and coconut shavings when I got off the plane in Santiago in the Dominican Republic. It was nine years earlier that my family had decided to create a new chapter in a new country. I never imagined the day I would go back to my people, where I belong.

As we walked out of the airport, I saw my Uncle Carlos (that's his middle name; his first name is very long and very difficult to pronounce). He still had the same white, crooked smile and the same motorcycle I used to ride on.

The first thing I did was hug him tight, leaving teardrops on his shirt.

"Te extrañé mucho," he said, making me cry even more.

After our long welcome-home hugs, we climbed inside his friend's Jeep. It only had five seats, and we were six in total (including his new wife, Ana, whom he mentioned a lot in his letters). As in any family tradition (or is it my family tradition?), the middle child must sit in the middle seat. But I kind of broke that rule because I wanted to see my house.

As we got ourselves comfy (well, tried), my uncle put an old mixtape he made for my mom, titled "Mi gente está allá," in the stereo. The music started playing, and everyone was doing a little dance in the jammed seat—except for me. I was looking at the stars and remembering the times I had before leaving: running after the ducks in my backyard, wearing my grandmother's jewelry and heels to make myself look older, the early mornings when I would wake up before the rooster woke the rest of the family and go to the top of the little mountain near our house just to see my grandfather cut the coconuts off the trees.

Snapping myself back to reality, I noticed all the small metal shacks that looked like parts from the Tin Man in *The Wizard of Oz*. After a couple more metal houses, we finally came to a stop at the white concrete house that was decorated with beautiful tropical flowers. While my uncle was reminding the family about the family rules, I hopped out of the Jeep and admired the house for a few seconds. I smelled the fresh air and told myself, "I'm finally home, where I belong."

---

*Medelin Cuevas (she/they) is a mother of a 2-year-old girl. In their spare time, she reads and engages in classes and programs to finish her Massage Therapy certification.*

# Ancestral Hunger Feeds on Hollow Memories

## by KAYLA MORGAN, 2023

*A free-verse poem about the bittersweetness of memories, childhood,
and sentimentality from an ancestral and familial perspective.*

As a child, I would peel layers of putrid pomegranates
and plant their forgotten savoriness in my soul. Sentimental,
for seasons of flavored fruit my body has never eaten.
My tongue craves beloved tastes under fatherly sun,
extracted from the nostalgic palm of motherly love—
where satisfaction is more than a childbearing promise,
but a kept birthright.

My spirit envisions lineages to be conservative, classically
unending. My fingers were never fermented in normalcy,
but my body can't help but believe in sanity, yet my throat
detests the disappointing scent of pomegranates.

Spring never once blossomed into my plate. No floral fruition
of familiarity, no blood blooming under the intimacy of spring.
I can only recall the grim of pollen, its aroma, unfair and unsettling.
When new beginnings feel like death, unsolicited blessings
like nightmares—when did pomegranates become so
rotten in their ambiguity?

I always envied grapefruit's enrichment in tartness unconstructed:
so bitter, but dances in our mouths with sweetness soaked
in pleasure; so alluring on the mind, but unnerving on the tongue;
so flavorful in its flaws, yet enticing in our memories—
this is what you call home.

My pomegranates do not need to be coated from honey nectar
woven in the embracement of mother nature: Supremacy,
untampered; tenderness, unparalleled; perfection, unquestioned.
All I need is for it to purely be.

I can handle sour charms, the sting of strange aftertastes.
But a rotting, decaying birthright is fatal. My bittersweet memories—
promised to me, and signed ancestrally, will satisfy my dying appetite.

*Kayla Morgan is a first year Middlebury College student from New York City pursuing a degree in Economics. She enjoys skiing down mountains, performing spoken word poetry, getting lost in museums, and taking pictures of beautiful things.*

## Tell Your Story

### A Prompt from Kayla Morgan

Think of something you uncannily feel sentimental about but have never truly experienced. Write down your immediate "recollections" and emotions—take the reader on a journey through your headspace.

# Color Me Gentle//False Healing

## by ALANTA THOMAS, 2019

*Love should be loud and bold, within graceful arm's length.*

Color me gentle
Fill in all my blank spaces
Use your colorful emotions and shower me
Use the color red to represent your love
And fill me up
Use a color of your choice
To represent the way you feed my mind
With knowledge and confidence in my future
Endeavors
Color me gentle
Color me forever
—alanta
I thought you were the key to healing
You wrapped my wounds
You stitched my lacerations
You sheltered me
You hid me from the world to keep me safe
You hid me so I wouldn't see
See what love really was
The wounds you wrapped I retrieved from you
The lacerations were cut deep at the hands of you
You feed me fear and torment
But at the end of the night, I still let you back in

---

*Alanta Thomas is just a 21-year-old girl making it in the city that never sleeps.*

# False Healing II

## By MARION RAI, 2023

*This piece is an attempt to juxtapose and twist the idea of "love"
that the first piece provided.*

alanta—
your skin is now curdled, as I paint
you in my favorite colors
red and blue and violet:
an amalgamation for a bruise and yet,
look
your body bears it like a fruit.
I see beauty that nobody else does. and
as colors bleed from your eyes:
seep into your body,
believe that you are my favorite art.

alanta—
at the end of the night, with you
subsumed by my brushstrokes,
i am a gleeful child.

*Marion Rai (she/her) is an Asian American writer who loves sushi and animated movies. You can find her at the library rereading* Pride and Prejudice *for the tenth time.*

## Tell Your Story

### A Prompt from Marion Rai

With the line "You hid me so I wouldn't see," Thomas's poem turns from the positive things the subject of the poem did to the negative ones. Think of a complicated relationship in your life. List the positive things that person did for you, letting it bleed into the double-edged things. Challenge yourself to see how those things coexist.

# Tell Your Story
## A Prompt from
## Abby West and Rebecca Carroll

Think of someone you know well. How would you go about helping them shape their narrative through the questions you ask, while still leaving room to elicit something new? Write down the person, the questions you would ask them, and why.

---

*Abby West is a recovering journalist and true pop culture junkie, whose decades at prominent media organizations such as* Essence, Entertainment Weekly, *and* People *have given her a love of stories that explore, empower, and celebrate underrepresented communities. She is a member of Girls Write Now's Editorial Advisory Committee and Vice President and Editorial Director at Amistad.*

---

*Rebecca Carroll is a writer, creative consultant, editor-at-large and host of the podcast Come Through with Rebecca Carroll: 15 essential conversations about race in a pivotal year for America (WNYC Studios). Her latest book,* Surviving the White Gaze: A Memoir, *was published in February and has been optioned by MGM Studios and Killer Films with Rebecca attached to adapt and executive produce for TV. Her podcast project, an Audible original called* Billie Was a Black Woman, *which Rebecca created, wrote and hosts was released in April 2021.*

# Chercher

by ROBERTA NIN FELIZ, 2014

*I heard you been looking for me.*

I've been lost the past year and some change
Because I wasn't accustomed
To change
Like spare change in my wallet
15 cents
One for every year I've lived

Under Sweet Gum trees far from
The hair-bleaching sun rays that alleviated
My nut brown hair with cinnamon streaks
In my mom's *pollo al orno*
In the squeaks of my pivoting basketball shoes
I search for me

I'm lost in every curl
zig zag, twist, wave, and coil on my head
Abundantly bouncing back
From the limp waves flat ironing rendered
Wandering between the strands of hair that
Still haven't decided whether or not they want to curl completely
And those that curl excruciatingly close to my scalp

Awaiting May
To search in rainbows
Semicircles decorating the sky of my hood
Rummaging beneath books and sandy beaches
Jeans, pens, journals, poems

Exploring the pupil in its entirety
I make my way through the eyes of those I love

In my mother's eyes
They're freshly brewed Café Bustelo brown
Their brown washed away with years of hurting for me
They were Curaçaoan coconut green, my ex-lover's eyes
His pupils shrinking with the lies he fed me
Black holes in which I could have easily been lost
I delved into lies feet first
Emerging in cinders with only one of my Adidas

When time speeds up
Like electrons when they absorb energy releasing light
*Plus lentement*, world

On days where I forget the French words
I forlornly flip through my notebook
Failing to find the French words for "I found me"
*Vien ici s'il vous plait*
Let me be found
Amongst the *accent aigus* of past participles
Hanging off the cedille of *Curaçao*
Or balancing on the accent *circonflex of être*
Whispering to the clouds
*Oui, Oui* "I heard you been looking for me"

---

*Roberta Nin Feliz is a writer from New York City. Her work has been featured in Broadly, MTV, and Bitch Media, among others. She holds a degree in Computer Science from the University of Pennsylvania.*

# Lost & Found
## by SHAMU W., 2023

*This is a poem about personal growth and finding yourself.*
*It's a grueling journey but one worth taking.*

I've been led to believe
that if I wanted something to happen,
it would just because I worked for it.

But now I know
Just how wrong they were.
It was all a *lie*.

I've tried to swallow my pride,
Hold my head up high,
And push past any doubts that form in the process.

It hurts to breathe or even think,
Knowing I'm trying my best—
Yet there's **no one** there to console or comfort me.

I want to say I'm proud of how far I've come
but I don't think I've ever felt satisfied with myself.
I wonder why that is…

It's not because I'm being hard on myself,
I like to think it's because I want to be humble.
But what does it mean to *be* humble?

Am I even visible?
What happens now?
I'm afraid that I'm not good enough.

Here I stand,
before a group of cynics and well—
It feels strange.

On one hand,
I know they're waiting for the moment I fail
The moment where I stumble and fall

But even when that does happen—
Should I crumble before them?
Truthfully, the answer hasn't presented itself yet.

I look amongst the sea of people
Hoping someone will finally see my efforts
Appreciate the work I've put in

But it feels impossible.
They say to follow the signs,
But what if those signs are sending mixed signals?

I think the problem is…
I've been yearning to be found—
Without realizing all I needed was **myself**.

I don't need to find my way yet.
I'm fine taking the long road.
Isn't that what life's about?

So yes, I may be young
and yes, I may be lost.
But sometimes it's better to find my own way.

And who knows,
maybe I'll finally be able to look at myself
and feel a sense of accomplishment.
Because after all,
Isn't that what life's about?

---

*Shamu W. (they/their) is a 19 year old college student with a passion for storytelling and art. They've been writing for a decade now and love to share their stories with the world.*

## Tell Your Story

### A Prompt from Shamu W.

When you hear the phrase: "take me with you," what emotions/memories does it invoke? Do you think of a specific person or people?

# Noriko's Postcards
## by MONA HADDAD, 2009

*Noriko traveled not only to explore, but also to escape.*

Noriko came to visit every few months or so, every time she took a break from her travels. She sent me postcards from all of her trips, and I'd collect them in her absence, tracking her trek across the globe from 86th Street, learning of Holland, of Japan, of Los Angeles. She came to see my mother, but I like to think she stayed for me. Every time she visited, she would play with me, going along with whatever my interests were at the time.

Once, we had a Bugs Bunny wedding. I was the bride, my giant Bugs Bunny stuffed animal was the groom, and she was the flower girl, the facilitator, and the guests, all at once. I couldn't find flowers, so we threw Band-Aids left and right as we marched down the aisle, setting the scene for my big day. We sang the Japanese children's songs she had taught me, and by the end of the afternoon, Bugs Bunny, who was dressed in the tuxedo he came with, went from the star of the wedding (second to me, of course) to a wallflower, as Noriko and I danced to my mother's records and ate Oreos at the reception.

Not long after, Noriko left again to travel, and did not return for years. I continued to receive postcards, but as time went on, the intervals between them grew further and further apart. Her last postcard came almost a decade after Bugs Bunny's wedding. She had written to tell me how she had decided to marry a real groom and to stay in Los Angeles for good. She attached pictures of her "children," two plush kittens named Jim and Aaron, and asked how my marriage was going. By then, Bugs Bunny no longer fit in my life or my room, which was covered with books and preteen possessions, and was boxed up and sent to storage.

Soon after, through a conversation with my mother, I learned that Noriko traveled, not only to explore, but also to escape. Born the daughter of a Japanese princess, she renounced her title upon rejecting her arranged marriage. She traveled the world to find a new home, I imagine, and sent me that last postcard when she finally found it, to let me know that she was okay and that everything that wasn't would soon be, too.

---

*Mona Haddad was born in New York. She attended the Hackley School in Tarrytown, New York and Mount Holyoke College in South Hadley, MA.*

# Like Noriko Did

## by RACHEL YOUNG, 2023

*Through this piece, I hope to honor the people who have added joy, love, and warmth to my childhood even though we are no longer together.*

I imagine Noriko had stored the life she renounced in the deepest recesses of her mind. She moved every few months to chase something resembling a home, or perhaps to escape something that didn't. Every day her reflection in the mirror was shrouded by steam and confusion. A decision that was supposed to be cleansing suddenly made life blurry and unclear. She couldn't seem to see herself anymore. Not in New York, Holland, Japan, or Los Angeles.

Every February, my grandmother would hold a Lunar New Year party that brought along the most distant of relatives and friends. Anyone looking for good food, a shared history, or the ability to reconnect in their mother tongue would come. I was always the youngest one there besides the toddlers, who played with all my old toys that were kept in storage at my grandparents' apartment: old Lego blocks, toy soldiers, and a Bugs Bunny stuffed animal that had once been my groom. It all seemed like a lifetime ago, compared to my current matrimony to the preteen acne smattered across my forehead and the books stacked in piles on the floor of my room.

In the years after Noriko stopped visiting, I would look for her in the crowd of guests and wonder if she would ever come back to be a part of my life. I had met her there years ago when I was seven. She had arrived at the party before everyone else. While my mother and grandmother were busy cooking in the kitchen, I felt grateful to have someone to indulge in my childhood interests. I was often the only one sitting in the living room so I liked to pretend the guests were coming to see me. I told Noriko I learned to make paper cranes in school and she taught me how to fold cups out of the scraps of paper on my grandmother's coffee table. I giggled when she raised her eyebrows and sipped water as quickly as she could from our delicate creations. I sometimes daydream about what she would say and what she would think of me now. My imagination was long ago packed away in storage, and Noriko with it.

There is all this love I have for Noriko that I can never act on. I can only play back memories like dreams when I'm surrounded by unfamiliar faces. Noriko's warm laughter rings through my mind again and I'm brought back to childhood. These daydreams unsettle my teenage foundations, and I fear I will never find peace about the pair we could've been. Even if this confusion never resolves, I hope to find peace. Someday I will find out for myself that everything that isn't okay now will be okay soon, like Noriko did.

*Rachel Young is a college student studying data science and business. You will often find her trying new recipes, getting lost in a new book, or spending time with her friends and family.*

## Tell Your Story

### A Prompt from Rachel Young

Write a piece about a person you knew from childhood that you don't or can't speak to now. Where do you think they are? What does their life look like?

*This conversation is between current Publishing 360 mentee
Rachel Young and mentor alumni Andrea Juncos, speaking on
behalf of Mona Haddad, her former mentee who passed away
in 2016. Read Mona's piece, "Noriko's Postcards", and Rachel's
response, "Like Noriko Did" on page 52.*

**RACHEL YOUNG:** It's incredible to tell those stories and I hope that through being able to revisit Mona's piece, we can also extend her voice to future generations. I'm sure that they will be just as inspired as I was when I first heard it.

I wanted to start the interview by asking you a little bit about yourself. Where did you grow up and what do you do for a living now?

**ANDREA JUNCOS:** I'm originally from a suburb of Philly called Westchester, but I moved to New York in 2001 after college. I lived there for twelve years, working in education, nonprofits, and workforce development. I had different jobs, including with the New York City Department of Education. I've always had this dual love for education and writing. In my first or second year in New York, I joined Girls Write Now. I was really seeking a community of writers and an opportunity to build my writing career, as well as trying to figure out if I wanted to be a teacher. It was cool to be able to teach some writing workshops for Girls Write Now.

Fast forward, I've had a lot of different career stops in education where I've used writing a lot. I worked at New York Law School as a Director of Communication and did some writing and editing in a marketing and communications role. But after a while, I felt ready to be closer to what I was writing about. I wanted to be part of the action a bit more.

I moved to Boston almost a decade ago to go to graduate school in Education Policy and Management. I've spent my career at non-profits, but I've been at the same non-profit for about eight years now. It's called Jobs For the Future, and it's a national organization focused on how we support people in economic advancement through both education and workforce development. I now do research and policy work that's focused on racial equity. It's awesome.

**RY:** That's super incredible because it relates to Girls Write Now in terms of advancing people with opportunities. Girls Write Now does a lot of work in terms of ensuring college is a supported process for young people, and that has been a really great resource for me and I'm sure a lot of other young writers, too. I'm wondering—how did you become a Girls Write Now mentor and what years were you a mentor?

**AJ:** I always laugh that my twenty-three-year-old self would probably not be accepted now into the program as a mentor. But I joined in 2002 and I was a mentor for seven years. When I joined Girls Write Now, it was not yet a non-profit. It was all volunteers. We didn't have a space. I remember meeting Maya, the Founder and Executive Director, in a coffee shop in Union Square for the first time. I brought my resume and writing samples, and she always used to tease me that I brought a lot of formality to the interview. But I didn't know what to expect. I certainly wasn't a seasoned writer at the time, but I was super interested in the community of women writers and young women.

I've seen quite a bit of change; that was twenty-five years ago. It's been really cool. I was with the organization for seven years of mentoring, and then I joined what was at the time called the Program Advisory Committee, helping with recruitment and enrollment. I was also on the Board of Directors, which was a great experience. And now I'm part of the diversity committee, and it's been cool to find a new way to be involved in the organization. I'm a lifetime supporter.

**RY:** That's really incredible, and we definitely appreciate the support. That's almost twenty-one years! You've been with Girls Write Now for practically my entire life. How have you seen Girls Write Now grow and change throughout the years and what kind of impact have you seen on young teen writers as the organization has continued to grow and develop itself?

**AJ:** I'm so impressed and inspired at the growth and longevity and sustainability of Girls Write Now. A lot has happened these twenty-five years. With the pandemic, and through all of these changes—I've just been so impressed. I mean, when I started it was so small. There were probably like twenty mentors then. But we kept growing and growing.

At the beginning, everything was just completely based on volunteers, and that was hard work. Maya is such a champion of this organization and how the organization has been able to grow and evolve and be flexible. Girls Write Now has also been strategic about growth. I remember a time where we got a lot of questions about expanding to new cities and the growth plan. There was a very intentional focus then of staying in New York and growing within New York with the number of students and mentors we can serve.

Now it's interesting that there's this virtual reach that's allowed the organization to grow. I'm really heartened by how much thought and intentionality there's been. Just the trajectory that the organization has been on is awesome. In terms of impact, I consider myself as impacted by the organization as a mentee. I've seen in all of us, mentors and mentees alike, an increase of confidence skills and comfort level with sharing your writing and trying new genres.

There's so much impact in terms of skills and confidence, but also with relationships. I had a very close relationship with Mona and the other mentees I've been partnered with. That's the most lasting part. I'm still friends with other mentors as well, and they're really an impressive group. We all celebrate each other. So there's impact there, too.

**RY:** In my experience from the mentee side, my mentor has impacted my life in ways I don't think I could ever repay them for. It's been an incredible experience.

I'm wondering, at the time you were working with Mona, what was going on in the world? Did that influence you in terms of what you worked on as a pair?

**AJ:** I was trying to think about that, because this is post-9/11 New York. We talked about 9/11 a little bit when I was there, but there's been an evolution of New York after that I'm thinking about.

I think Mona and I showed up best in our writing with what was going on emotionally in our lives. We would meet in a Barnes & Noble on the Upper East Side and write about what we saw and what we were experiencing. We wrote a lot about high school experiences. And New York, and what it is like to live in New York. It was so interesting to me because I come from a background of growing up in the suburbs and I was new to New York, and Mona was born and raised in New York City. There was a lot about what it means to be a young woman in New York City.

**RY:** Definitely. I was wondering, what do you remember about writing Noriko's Postcards with Mona? What was the inspiration for that?

**AJ:** I looked back in my old Yahoo inbox and just typed the word Noriko in to try to find it. Mona first sent me a draft in an email, but I think she started it at a workshop that I couldn't attend as I was out of town for a wedding. She was like, *oh, here is something that I wrote. It's not that good.* She had a tendency to downplay the talent she had.

What I remember is that she first had just a mind dump—a stream-of-consciousness writing of all these memories. I had inserted some comments and sent it back to her, and I was like, this is amazing. This is so interesting. My feedback consisted mostly of questions. Tell me more. Who is this person and why are they sending you postcards? What did they mean to you?

**RY:** Thank you for sharing that. When I was reading Mona's pieces, I thought they were so cool and creative. I think her pieces are wonderful. I wonder if Mona ever mentioned where she typically got her ideas or inspiration from?

**AJ:** That's a great question. She had such an active and creative mind. She was constantly coming up with ideas. She read a lot. She didn't even understand why people watch TV shows. She was like, I don't get it. It's so boring. She had a love of music as well. She came from a musical family and that was something we shared and bonded over.

She was just very hungry and eager to create. She found inspiration in everything. She was a very exceptional person with a very active mind. There was a lot of what was on her mind informing what she was creating.

**RY:** You know, it's really cool. Just reading her pieces, you can tell how talented she was. How these ideas come from a place that's, like, pure talent, but also from all the time that she dedicated to her various interests. It was so cool to get to read them and get inspiration from her in my own reflection. I love the way she describes things. I was like, wow. All of these memories seem so vivid. And I can relate to them.

**AJ:** One thing I would add about her inspiration is that she was a very good student. She was really interested in psychology and dreams, and there's some threads of that that show up in her work as well.

**RY:** Definitely. In the artistic process, what was that experience like, to meet at Barnes & Noble and talk through your sessions?

**AJ:** We had the privilege of having both these monthly in-person writing workshops and the weekly in-person meeting. I'm thinking of a picture that somebody took of Mona and I at a workshop. We're both looking down, writing, and both smiling to ourselves because we were getting into whatever the prompt was.

There's something really cool about being in this huge room that suddenly goes really quiet when everyone is writing. Can you really get into your own world around other people? That takes some getting used to. You can't turn your camera off and your sound off. But we both found the workshops really inspiring and motivating once you established that trust first.

In our one-on-one meetings, we probably met at six p.m. or something like that. We liked to chat for a while, and then we would do some writing. We had some readings to anchor us. We were working towards something that gave us the motivation and accountability to write. That was really helpful. We could have talked a bunch, but it was helpful to have questions about what came out of workshop or what we should do for a pair reading.

Even after we were an official mentee-mentor pair, we were still in each other's lives and sending each other writing. There was usually something that was prompting us to write together, like an essay for a new class or whatever. It was cool to have that balance of talking about life and having it show up in our writing, too.

**RY:** Reading the short story after all this time, has your perspective on it changed?

**AJ:** Well, yeah. When I went back to look at our original exchange, it was cool to see the evolution. I saw the growth even within that piece. There's an innocence to it that I feel like is time specific and shows a fascination or view of an older person that is traveling around. Mona traveled quite a bit with her family; she has family in Turkey and South America. But I think she had this idea that we all probably grow up with, which is that we need to get married and settle down. That comes up in this piece, and I think it's an interesting viewpoint into how you look at your childhood and what's important to you at the time.

**RY:** I really appreciate that perspective. I think about how my younger cousins live such a different life than I did. They have cell phones as soon as they're in third grade and digital things are all around them. It's interesting to share what effect Mona's childhood influences had on her and what that looked like.

I was sorry to hear after choosing her piece that she passed away, and that she can't be with us today to share her voice and create more things and be a part of her life. Is there anything you'd like to say to memorialize her in this book?

**AJ:** I appreciate that. Part of why I'm so excited to talk to you is because I want people to know about Mona. I'm heartened that her work is being shared. She really was a prolific writer. She wrote so much, and the world has not seen most of it. I'm glad that even one snippet of her writing can be shared and memorialized here because I will never forget her and I don't want anyone else to forget her.

She was a really incredible person, and so creative. She was so original. She saw things in a totally different way, and she really had no concept of how unique she was. I think she would be so touched that you found her piece and that it resonated with you or inspired you. That's what she was writing for—to make herself and other people feel less alone.

# WRITING
# AND
# PUBLISHING
# TIPS

# WRITING TIPS

### *What can I do when I feel stuck and the words aren't coming to me?*

"I may not be inspired by anything, but what if I write about my hair? How long does it take my hair to grow? When did I start disliking my hair? Why is other people's hair different from mine? Now you have questions and things to research. They may not have been things that were pressing on your heart but they're things that allow you to be exploratory. Being a student of your craft is being able to explore and find things that you love or that you didn't think you cared about. When you really have writer's block, my shortened answer to getting over it is to go on Netflix and watch films about the ocean or animals. What happens in the ocean seems to be the most poetic thing ever".

— **JASMINE MANS**, Girls Write Now Teaching Artist, poet, and author of *Black Girl, Call Home*

"Re-read your favorite piece of fiction. Watch your favorite TV show or movie and really pay attention to the writing. Listen to your favorite songs and focus on the lyrics. Consuming published material helps you break through writer's block and reconnect with the words and how they flow together to create something magical."

— **RACHEL PRATER**, Girls Write Now Mentor, writer, and editor

"Your writing should not be homework. Start with a blank page again. Rinse and repeat until you don't hate it. So much of writing is psychological more than craft."

— **BRIT BENNETT**, Girls Write Now Teaching Artist and author of *The Vanishing Half*

"When I'm working on a book, I pick a playlist or CD that I love for that book. I'm a big fan of the Pomodoro technique, so even when the words aren't really flowing, I'll put in my headphones, set a timer for twenty-five minutes, and remind myself that I'm not going for perfection, that I just want to get something down. It's much easier to improve upon something versus nothing."

— **REBECCA LOWRY WARCHUT**, Girls Write Now Mentor and author of *Catastrophe Theory*

### *How can I create compelling characters that people want to read about?*

"I feel when my characters are struggling with tough decisions or faced with tough choices, it's a really great way to show character. You want them to be realistic and impactful and you want their behavior and their decisions to be impactful, it really helps if they do have something to wrestle with because it really shows their character. How they handle it. Whether it's in a good way or bad way if they make the right choices. Putting them in these situations where they have to dig themselves out really shows the reader what they're like. It gives them a deeper look inside the character. I love to put my characters in these very tough situations."

— **SABINA KHAN**, Girls Write Now Teaching Artist
and author of *Zara Hossain Is Here*

"I'm always more interested in people than moving them around a chessboard. If you're thinking about the character, then they're going to do things and our job is to fill out that world and follow them or lead them and that's what's more interesting to me. I mean, I like a good car chase, too, but if I have a choice, it's always gonna be about the human drama."

— **NATALIE BASZILE**, Girls Write Now Teaching Artist
and author of *Queen Sugar*

"Your characters don't have to be "relatable", and worrying about whether readers will relate to them is a surefire way to block yourself as you write. To write fully fleshed-out characters, you have to understand exactly who they are: imagine an external pressure on them, and make sure you can fully articulate how they would react. And individual characters' voices should be distinctive: in a page of unattributed dialogue, we should be able to tell who is speaking at any given moment."

— **ELIZABETH MINKEL**, Girls Write Now Mentor,
writer, editor, and podcast host

"Write about characters that you want to read. They should mirror real people, have a solid backstory, quirks as well as great qualities. They need to have a challenge that the reader is rooting for them to overcome."

— **DONNA HILL**, Girls Write Now Mentor Alum and author of
*After the Lights Go Down* and *Confessions in B-Flat*

*How can I write a first line or sentence that really pulls
the reader into my piece?*

"The Hook: Have a great opener that situates us right in the middle of the action. You can use dialogue, proclaim a want, or make a statement."

— **SUSANNA HORNG**, Girls Write Now Teaching Artist,
NYU Clinical Professor, and Jerome Hill
Artist Fellow in Literature

"Start in the middle of the action. Cut out the unnecessary introduction and jump straight to the obstacle a character needs to overcome. You can introduce them and the setting through actions and dialogue!"

— **RACHEL PRATER**, Girls Write Now Mentor,
writer, and editor

"Novels, I think, are really interesting when you start out with a problem."

— **BRIT BENNETT**, Girls Write Now Teaching Artist and
author of *The Vanishing Half*

"Pretend you only have 30 seconds to get someone to listen to your story. What type of things would you say to get their attention quickly?"

— **SAMANTHA RESNIK**,
Girls Write Now Mentor and writer

*Visit www.girlswritenow.org/resources for more*

# PROFESSIONAL WRITING TIPS

## *What kind of jobs are available for writers?*

"Tons! Editors at publishing companies, Human Resources, teaching, law, content writing, blog writing, television, and news. Every business needs people that can write!"

— **DONNA HILL**, Girls Write Now Mentor Alum
and author of *After the Lights Go Down*
and *Confessions in B-Flat*

"Every professional job requires solid communication and writing skills! A good way to find out where you want to land is to look for internships that interest you. Then you'll know what's a good fit for where you want your career to go."

— **RACHEL PRATER**, Girls Write Now Mentor,
writer, and editor

## *How can I get short stories, poems, and essays published?*

"For shorter pieces, start with literary magazines! There are zillions, and many of them focus on specific identities, age groups, themes, etc. Duotrope is a great database."

— **LIVIA NELSON**, Girls Write Now mentor and writer

"Submit to literary magazines, journals, and other publications! If you aren't sending out your work, you can't be published. And a big part of the writing life is letting rejection roll off your shoulders; lots of experience submitting is how you get comfortable with the nos and smarter about where your yeses are likely to come from."

— **MARISA SIEGEL**, Girls Write Now Mentor
and author of *Fixed Stars*

"Reach out to as many people as possible and don't give up after continued rejection."

— **SAMANTHA RESNIK**, Girls Write Now
Mentor and writer

## SELF-REFLECTION PROMPTS:

*How do you feel when you begin a new creative project? Do you experience excitement thinking of the endless possibilities of your creation? Do you feel pressure to express yourself in a certain way? Write a letter to a new project telling it how you feel and what you hope it will become.*

*How does it feel to call yourself a writer? What does that word mean to you?*

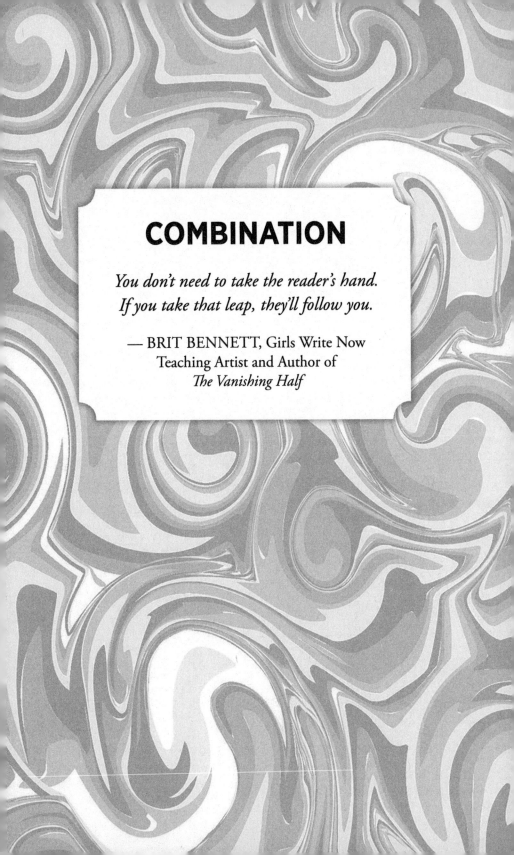

# COMBINATION

*You don't need to take the reader's hand.*
*If you take that leap, they'll follow you.*

— BRIT BENNETT, Girls Write Now
Teaching Artist and Author of
*The Vanishing Half*

# Who Am I

by CARMIN WONG, 2013

*This piece communicates my struggle for representation a decade earlier, and I was reluctant to share it, thinking it was too personal and that no one would understand. Michelle Chen proved to me otherwise. I hope that we continue to turn to language to bravely claim our insecurities and find visibility in the writings of others.*

In 2000, I moved to the United States with my parents and sisters. We lived with my paternal family, who had already moved to the states, before getting a place of our own. My maternal family did not obtain visas to join us, though they tried.

*Indian.* A name I have been given all my life. Because my mother is called a "c*olie." A stereotype given to South and East Asian descendants. Folks whose ancestors were carried across the ocean in forced servitude. I reject that name.

My father is Black. Meaning, our people were forcibly brought to the Americas through enslavement and involuntary labor. I come from a bloodline of ancestors who have found resistance dwelling in their bones.

Both of my parents are Guyanese, though. Folks say they look different from each other. And I look more like my mother. I look different from my dad and his sisters. I have heard that from them, too. Enuf times to wish my flesh could know a different residence.

*Different.* A word I cannot unhear. A word that reminds me there is no ground fertile enuf for the undesired. What do I tell them? What do I tell each side of my family?

I wish I looked like them both. Had their styles. Had their figures. A reason to stop being labeled by any name but my own.

I wish I could tell them how this amount of invisibility feels, how folks who exclude one-half of you will always try to keep you at arms-length, or how all I ever wanted was to fit in. With my own family. Just for a day.

We lived in Queens, New York, home to corner stores and Chopped Cheese. My first high school was in Queens, where security guards patrolled the hallways and my teacher would call my parents from work when I was late to class. One time, I had a substitute teacher call me Ghetto.

*Exotic.* That's what the kids my age call me. A stereotype, a micro-aggression, a slight of a tongue, a disguise. A way to point out our differences.

I used to think that was a kind of exaltation. I used to think it was a kind of greeting—for the unnamed. Because I heard it all my life—in school, on buses, in the subway.

It took me no time to learn that it wasn't a compliment. Instead, it is a way to say I see you but can't make sense of *what* you are.

I deserve a name I can answer to. We all deserve a name we can answer to. Not a reminder of when we are foreign to everyone else.

Should I correct them? If that means I could fit in. Just for a day.

**When I was in college, my cousins came to visit me at school. The security guard asked for identification. They wanted two proofs: that they were my cousins, and that this is my name.**

I have to check a box. They want to know who I am. They see my last name, they assume to know me. *She's definitely Asian. So, what side of your family is Chinese?* It's like having an unfamiliar teacher doing the attendance all over again. Should I correct them?

*An Indian, exotic, Chinese girl?*

I still haven't checked a box . . . Maybe I will never fit in. Not even for a day.

---

*Carmin Wong (she/her/We) is a poet, playwright, educator, and PhD student at Penn State University. Her artistry and teaching invokes a tradition of Black feminist praxis. She is a devoted aunt, sister, daughter, and friend.*

# Name Games

## by MICHELLE CHEN, 2023

*Traveling across oceans and lifespans, diasporic identity struggles
are beautifully illustrated through new mythological combinations
that provide a lifeline for understanding the narrator's multiple names,
as well as a trailway for the process of grief.*

*for* 美美新 *(chén měi xīn)*

My name didn't (used to) speak easily—pinyin twin
dice scattered upon a losing deck—spades for both war & garden,
hearts sliced out from the Janus-bodied fish-lion of Temasek
& a bald-faced raptor piercing through coasts like the needle
of my mother's mother stitching dollar bills into my underwear
& coat pockets before flashing into cinders, incense, overripe oranges,
marble, yellow tissue paper coins offered to warm her soul in an Eden
beyond her understanding. My name descendant of Beowulf's dragon,
strokes forgotten-soft in ashy footprints on sallow earth, a hero's
godly final destination. I have inherited his slayer's love for fame &
kindness to his people, hallucinations of gold burning in chips red
& black, for my ancestors' dreams humble & bold, desires buzzing
—in fluorescents, pouring whiteness into midnight afterparties.
My countries, in their meet-cute, left these banquets without their stars.
Did they fight over the bill or go Dutch?
Being spoken is trying to split quartz with a stone more impure
than an axe of a tongue whittled from a stake where a woman
hung before being consumed by ashes &
a fanged serpent mated with a glistening dragon.
Is the phoenix Greek or Chinese? Is the phoenix
yin or yang? A yang woman meets mare through a dating app
& they birth centaurs like how the gods birthed Muses
countless and unstoppable, how throwing the scarlet pouch of a name
upwards creates ripples of ecstasy, salt floating to the
surface of a disturbed sea.
My name is scattered-sweet in beads of liquid nitrogen ice cream

clinging to a stainless steel wok, biology teacher leaning forward
to sing Michelle, my belle, Michelle my belle when seeing me cry.
Chang'e stole the drug of immortality to save a foreign warrior
with an iron grip
—leaving my grandmother beneath pond shallows, Ophelia's
searchers' shadows—singeing dangling moss, thicker than witches' shawls.
The Jade Emperor's ten suns reach Denmark to play-fight, evaporating
tears, oceans straight out below hulls of lost ships, shuffling fortune and
luck.
One by one the cards flip, inked with 新加坡 / 美国 / Xīn Jiā Pō / Měi Guó
Singapore / America / Lion City / Beautiful Country—
crystals split & welded,
our surnames never change until they do. My name beckons
& leaves me stranded, over & over, a mirage of heat, guardians
of soil & sand. If spoken—come and speak—
turn any specks of dust (into) sentient beings.

---

*Michelle Chen is graduating from Stony Brook University this year with the same love for paper mail, warm zephyrs, and fried noodles, as well as Inspiring Girls Expeditions, Juniper Young Writers Workshop, and the Iowa Young Writers' Studio.*

## Tell Your Story

### A Prompt from Michelle Chen

Combine the most important myth you know
with what you imagine is the favorite mythology
of the first stranger you see, and free write
for twenty minutes.

# Las Manos de mi Mama
## by JAZMINE FLORENCIO, 2021

*My whole life I have been fascinated with my mother's
hands and how they are changing over time.
I decided to dedicate a poem to them.*

Dry, cracked, hard.
These hands, once soft,
Now long for attention.

Years ago they changed my diapers,
Soft and moisturized, they greeted me in the mornings
And tucked me in at night.

My mom's hands prepared hot coffees for years at our family's bakery.
They packed orders and stocked fridges,
Her bare fingertips flipped tortillas over the scorching stovetop,
and our tiny kitchen filled with that smoky aroma I grew up with.
Her hands heated up my own little hands on cold New York City winter days,
Squeezing them to remind me that I was safe.

But now her hands no longer function like they used to.
Once filled with life, her hands are drying up.
Now, her hands change my little sister's diapers.
And now I am the one who warms her dry, cracked hands in mine.

---

*Jazmine Florencio is a writer from New York City who is proud of her Mexican roots. She often writes about people who are underrepresented, including people of color and mothers. She wants to use her voice to bring attention to those who are often forgotten in the eyes of society.*

# Ring with the Pearl

## BY MAYA CRUZ, 2023

*Much like Jazmine Florencio, my mother's hands have always
stood out to me. They remind me of the saying "the more things
change, the more they stay the same…"*

I've got these hands that
Aren't really mine.
Wrinkled and slender-pinkied,
Thumbnail just like Mama's.

To her, this thumbnail is Gran's.
I don't know whose it was before Gran.
I wish Gran could tell me all about whose thumbnail she has.
Time leaves traces and no one who can explain.

Despite this unknowing,
I carry little pieces of woman-before-Gran
And woman-before-woman-before-Gran
In fingers and rings
From Mama that fit just so.

"Hands of a seal,"
"Hands like a spider."
Whose hands do I have?

Pearl placed on
A band that's not mine,
But will only fit me.
So, I treat it like something made to fit
But equally made to give away

Once, I lost it.
Tossed in the wash,
it waited in my jacket pocket;
I warmed my hands
And washed my clothes
Without knowing how close it was.
I was so afraid it was gone.

After about a year,
When I'd almost forgotten it was missing,
My mom opened her wrinkled palm,
Unfurled her slender pinky.
"Look what I have."

---

*Maya Cruz is a New York City–born-and-raised daughter, sister, and student. She has a burning passion for the arts and the overlap they have with the natural world.*

## Tell Your Story

### A Prompt from Maya Cruz

Tell the story behind a family heirloom. What would it say?
Where has it been? Who has worn it?

# Tell Your Story
## A Prompt from
## Daphne Palasi Andreades

Think about someone you love, or a character you are working on, whom you love. Write down as many specific details, images, and memories about this person or character, as you can from the point-of-view of somebody who loves them.

Now that you've completed this first part, let's move on to the second part: write about this same person from the point-of-view of someone who hates them.

Include specific details, images, and examples, as well. If "hate" is too strong a word, allow yourself to imagine why someone would dislike, be annoyed by, or find this person flawed.

---

*Daphne Palasi Andreades was born and raised in Queens, New York. She holds an MFA from Columbia University, where she was awarded a Henfield Prize and a Creative Writing Teaching Fellowship. She is the recipient of a Bread Loaf Writers' Conference scholarship, among other honors.* Brown Girls *is her first novel.*

# Dear You

## by JULIA MERCADO, 2015

*Ever had the worst year of your life? Back in 2015, it was 2011,*
*so I needed to tell past me that everything was going to be okay.*

Dear You,

You are the one who never washed your hair, wore the same sweater every day and smiled wide with blue braces. You are the one that bad days are based on. I feel we need to talk and now's the chance.

I know you. I know every detail about you, from your crazy obsessions to your favorite shade of blue. From Julia to Julia, from silent to outspoken. I never wanted to write to you. I never knew how because it's near impossible to talk to the ghosts that haunt you at night. The ghosts that make me get up out of sleep and write are the ones that affect me the most.

This letter makes me feel like I'm back at my therapist's office and she's having me analyze my life. She asked me to draw my family once.

I drew the mother, the father and you. Having no artistic abilities, I was ashamed to show my work to my therapist. I smiled a small smile and she frowned. Immediately, there was something wrong.

"What happened to the ears?" she asked. "Does no one listen to you?" Not one person on the paper had ears. I had often told her I had issues trying to get people to listen to me. I didn't think it would affect my drawing. I never think about ears when looking at people. Ears tend to be invisible if I'm not looking at them directly. As a therapist, she made me think about it more.

I didn't want to think about it more. I didn't want to have to think about times where I was you. That blue sweater is long gone from my closet but not far off in my memory. It reminds me of times when ears and voices were hard to see and hear.

I remember having nightmares where I couldn't speak to save my life. I could feel myself scream and no sound would come out. I always wondered what that meant to me and it dawned on me: I never speak up.

Throughout my younger years, I stayed quiet and let things play out, but I remember times before you where I didn't do that. My "friends" made fun of a classmate named Tiffany all the time. I stayed with them to look cool; that way they wouldn't make fun of me. It was the only way to stay safe from humiliation in that class. It wasn't fair that I did this when she was always being humiliated.

They viewed Tiffany as this monster who always had a limp and a school aide with her. It was horrible. Their faces turned red with laughter every time she would walk to throw out her trash with her aide. They pretended to be her and stared into the air with blank faces.

"I think there's something wrong with her brain. She's always staring into space," they would say.

One day, they were laughing so much that spit from their mouths landed all over me; I had to get up to move. I feel like that was the best thing I had ever done in my life. "I don't want to be over there," were the words that sparked a major turning point in your life. I still remember the look of confusion on her face when I said that. Neither of us knew what effect this moment would have on us. According to you, the only thing I'm good at is being awkward. Tiffany always sees the opposite in me. She believes in me. Even when I was you, she was there for me. She saw the beauty past the insecurity and the mute voice. Tiffany knew I was better than you, the one cocooned in awkwardness. I had lost my spunk for a while, but somehow Tiffany knew it would come back. She remembered the girl who did her own thing instead of letting people walk all over her. You are the part of me that is afraid to speak up. You let people say what they wanted to say about you. You believed their rash thoughts about you. I do not want to be you anymore. I still do not speak up and then I realize my day could have been better if I told at least one person how I truly felt. Believing in yourself is hard because everyone around you is judgmental. Who cares? Only you should care about what YOU do and what YOU say. People want to hear you, so speak loud and clear.

Whenever that past girl haunts you in your dreams, I want you to crack open this letter and read it again: out loud, in your head, or in song, until you absolutely get tired of what is in here and the message has finally gotten through. I would wish you luck in believing in yourself, but that's already beginning. You're making yourself heard in this moment, Little Miss. Keep going.

Yours Truly,
You (with a voice)

---

*Julia Mercado (she/her) is an entertainment writer and recruiter based in Queens. When she's not writing, she's podcasting and reminiscing about her time with Girls Write Now.*

# It Won't Last This Way

## by RUBY FAITH HENTOFF, 2023

*Do you ever wish you could turn back time...*
*and do everything differently?*

Dear Middle School Me,

It will get better. No matter what they say, or what they think of you, it will get better. When the new kid you befriended locks you out of a Houseparty room, and, when you ask to join, she writes "we're not friends anymore," ignore her. When your closest friends start going places without you and lie about it, ditch them. When you're curled up on your rug, a fresh radiator burn searing through your left arm, remind yourself: it won't last this way.

When you're regaining your senses after a seizure and realize that you're standing in the middle of a red-light Broadway street, calm down. When your teacher humiliates you in front of the entire class, talk to her. When your best friend starts tailing the "popular kids" and doesn't look at you in the halls, say something. Reach out to him. It doesn't have to last this way.

When you're watching *Heartlake City*, don't start crying because the real world is nothing like it. When you're cautioned not to play video games, don't spend five hours a day playing Run 3 on your Chromebook. That is also something you will come to regret. Be patient and remember, it won't last this way.

When none of your classmates want you in their group for the next Humanities project, don't take it personally. When your best Boomwriter chapter loses once again, don't take it to heart. When your math teacher starts teaching seventh graders about matrices and geometry, don't think that you're stupid for not understanding. You know that "school for the gifted" only means "school for the rich and conceited." But in a few years you'll finally be in a public school, and it won't last this way.

When your teacher fails you for an assignment you submitted one day late, fight back. When your friend refuses to address the cruel words he punctured you with, fight back. When you can't think or talk and you're scared, and you're telling yourself it'll always be like this, fight back, because that isn't true. It never was. You just didn't know it at the time.

When your best friend finally drifts out of sight, don't let him disappear in the clouds. Reach out. Break the wall with compassion. Stop clinging onto these fraudulent friends who bully you and tease you until your throat is numb. Cut them off. You don't want them and they don't want you. Embrace rejection. Appreciate exclusion. It will teach you what's fake from real. You will find something that lasts.

Nothing stays the same forever. You thought this cage you were locked in would never break. Even now, as my fingers sweep across the keys, I can feel myself back in middle school, running my fingers through the faux grass, holding my breath, longing to be free. And one day, you will be, too.

Love,

You (who learned)

*Ruby Faith Hentoff is a playwright, screenwriter, songwriter, and novelist graduating high school in the spring of '23. Between moments of inspiration, she loves to play piano, guitar, saxophone, and sing.*

## Tell Your Story

### A Prompt from Ruby Faith Hentoff

Find a partner and have each of you select a picture from your childhood. You'll start by writing what you see when you look at your own picture without showing it to the other person. Then, switch photos and repeat. When you're both finished writing, read each other's perspective about the photos. What emerges from your various perspectives?

# Loving in New Ways

by AVA NADEL, 2013

*Relationships don't need to be built on much.*

"*¿Cuantos años tienes tú, Norma?*" "*Dos.*"

*Dos?* I thought. *That's odd. Norma had to be older than 16.* Later that night, after dinner, my homestay mother told me that Norma has an intellectual disability: she is twenty-eight and doesn't know how to read or write.

Because my Spanish wasn't entirely perfect, I was unsure of how I should go about communicating with Norma. I had tried conversing with her using my Spanish, but even then, she seemed not to understand basic phrases I was saying. So, I sat there, at the dining table, shelling the lima beans for dinner. I could feel her staring at me, smiling as I plopped the shelled beans into a bowl. She then stuck one of them in front of my face. I had put the unshelled lima bean into the bowl with the shelled ones. She started laughing both with her mouth and eyes, and I did the same. We may not have been communicating using words, but using our emotions was enough.

For the next four days, I didn't feel so nervous around Norma anymore. I found that just by smiling and laughing, we could read each other's minds just fine. The next few mornings, I would be applying sunscreen in the bedroom and she'd come in, freshly showered, combing her silky, long black hair. We'd sit there in silence, taking care of ourselves separately, but fully aware of the other's presence. Much as I had when peeling the lima beans, I found that if I pulled off humorous actions, we'd improve our communication. I would play around with the stray dogs and cats and have her try and throw food in my mouth. One way or another she'd burst into a fit of giggles.

Through forming this sisterly bond with Norma with hardly any speaking, I learned perhaps one of the most valuable life lessons that any teenager could learn at my age: relationships don't need to be built on much. Norma and I surrounded each other with smiles and laughter and I came to realize that positive energy and emotions were all we needed.

The last morning of my homestay, my homestay mother, Carmela, was cooking us breakfast. Norma turned up the radio, humming along to what I assumed was her favorite song. She took me by the hands and started dancing with me. I could feel the tears welling up in my eyes—the tears I refused to let fall because I knew that if I showed her how weak I was, I wouldn't be able to explain it.

I miss her. I miss her cooing at the stray cat underneath the dining table. I miss her combing her wet hair as she watched me spray sunscreen on my mosquito bites before I left to weed the garden. I miss the dimples in her cheeks from when she'd get herself into a fit of giggles and couldn't stop laughing.

Sometimes the best love is the one that can exist without words.

---

*Ava Nadel was born in New York. She attended the Millennium High School in New York and Guilford College in Greensboro, North Carolina.*

# The Tide

## by LILIANA HOPKINS, 2023

*Last semester I was a volunteer for the Intercultural Partners Program. Once a week I practiced conversational skills with non-native English speakers. I met a kindred spirit, who revealed to me where language falters.*

Derya is standing outside the English Language Center. It's Tuesday, 10:30 in the morning. This is the fourth or fifth appointment we've had.

She smiles from ear to ear when she sees me. I breathe a little deeper and slip into the space between us. We walk side by side into the office together, as if we've done this a thousand times before.

"I waited out here for you! There is a girl in there who I can't—I have trouble . . . getting into conversations with her." Her eyes are smiling at me, hands creating a picture for every verb. "How is everything?"

After we sign in, we sit at our usual seats in the middle of the classroom. I study the assortment of earrings along her right ear. Ever since she pointed it out to me, I look for the star tattoo circling her lowest ear piercing.

"I am so tired! I slept bad last night." She sighs. "I woke up . . . 5:30? I couldn't go back to sleep."

I lean in, frowning. "Why?"

"I am a Scorpio. It could be because . . . I have . . . The moon this week is . . . uh . . . the sun, you know how it . . . " She cups her palm over her fist.

I wait a moment, allowing her space to find the words herself, before offering, "There is an eclipse in Scorpio moon."

"Yes! I couldn't wake up at the normal time," she sighs.

Derya's Turkish cadence reminds me of my mom's Russian accent. Something boiling underneath, pushing words up and out so that they thud on the table between us. She might be the same age as my mom. There is a softness around her eyes, grooves carved by all the shapes of love she's known.

"How is your reading assignment going?" I ask.

"It is soooo hard!" We take a huge breath together, laughing.

The "ooo" curves down, the same way my mom leans into her soooo's and I know's and ohhhhh's.

"There is all this . . . " Her hand pushes down on her shoulder.

I see the word on the tip of her tongue.

I smile. "Pressure?"

"Yes!"

"Words are too small, right?" I'm gesturing widely. "It's like each word is a tiny box, and somehow you have to put all the right ones together to create this unexplainable idea or experience."

"Ahhh, I want to explain things like this." Her hands flutter around her head. "Not like this!" Her hand stiffens, fingers lined up together. She aims a fake karate chop at the table.

"Sometimes when I think too hard about writing, it feels like math. It's so technical...linear..." I trail off, watching her eyes. Whenever they narrow, I know that I must be more visual so that we understand each other.

"They're both different ways to put the world into little boxes." I box up the air with my hands and rest the invisible boxes on the table. "But the more you do it, the simpler it gets."

"It takes a lot of time. And I'm always soooo tired. There are so many things to do."

"How's everything else?"

She pauses, taking her time to find the right words, before realizing there are never enough.

"Busy," she settles with, her eyes widening to increase the magnitude of the busyness. "Just... everything, you know?"

I nod. We empty our sighs and muses into the open air between us. I think about my mom's unread texts on my phone, the density of her.

Derya and I allow the silences to deepen the space between us. The words come and go. The tide of conversation rolls back and forth. We rest in the peace of listening and being heard, the language sparkling on the waves, nothing more than a trick of the sun. There is an ocean of understanding beneath us.

---

*Liliana Hopkins is a college student studying biology. You'll find her hidden in the library. She'll have her headphones on and a nineteenth century novel over her chemistry homework. She's probably listening to Outkast.*

## Tell Your Story

### A Prompt from Liliana Hopkins

Write a scene for a play or a screenplay that shows the depth of a relationship without dialogue. What kind of body language do the characters exhibit? How do they interact with each other and their environment?

# Tell Your Story
## A Prompt from Natalie Baszile

Write about a time, real or imagined, when you
really wanted something and either you or someone
else stopped yourself from getting it.

What did you say? How did you act? What do you wish
you'd said? How do you wish you could have behaved?

Imagine the same scene from before, but from the other
person's point of view. What were they thinking?
How were they feeling? Why didn't they want you
to have what you wanted?

---

*Natalie Baszile is the author of* Queen Sugar, *which has been adapted for television by Ava DuVernay and Oprah Winfrey. Natalie is a resident at SFFILM where she is working on a number of projects including GOOD PEOPLE, a narrative film adapted from her novel-in-progress. Natalie has had residencies at Ragdale Foundation, VCCA, Hedgebrook, and Djerassi, where she was the SFFILM and Bonnie Rattner Fellow. Her nonfiction work has appeared in O,* The Oprah Magazine, Lenny Letter, The Bitter Southerner, National Geographic *and numerous anthologies. Natalie lives in San Francisco with her family.*

# The Places We Came From
## by TASHI SANGMO, 2009

*A place now resides in my memory.*

In the place I am from, the land is evergreen and wide-open and decorated with colorful flowers in summers. The snowy mountains reach high up to the clear blue sky. The memory of cool, icy breezes in the early morning on my face never dies. I was born into a nomadic family like most people in my village, living on the mountains with domestic animals like yaks and sheep, and migrating to find places where there was enough water and grasses for the animals.

✳✳✳✳✳✳✳✳

In our village, houses were made of stones and timbers, with dry logs piled up around the house to make a fence. When smoke was coming from the chimney, I could tell that the house was not empty. Dusty, narrow streets stretched out from each house, and people and animals walked by every day, kicking up dirt.

✳✳✳✳✳✳✳✳

I was born when the land of Tibet had been snatched by Communist China, in 1959, and the Dalai Lama and half of the Tibetans were forced to escape to India as refugees.

Thousands of monasteries, nunneries, and education centers were destroyed, and millions of Tibetans lost their lives asking for more rights and freedom. Families left behind in Tibet were afraid to have any discussions on political issues. I was kept from understanding the politics and history of Tibet until I escaped over the mountains to India when I was eight years old.

✳✳✳✳✳✳✳✳

Life in the 1990s was pure and narrow: day and night. I knew only the world around me. I had no fears about what would happen in the future, since I was 100 percent sure that what I saw around me was everything there was in the world. I woke up every day with the same illiterate schedule before the red sun rose behind the mountains.

I wandered all day on the mountains along with the animals, waiting for the shadow of the trees to reach over the river so that I could go back home and play hide and seek with neighborhood friends. We kids liked rolling in the mud and clay until our clothes got wet and stuck to our bodies, despite the fact that we knew we'd be scolded by our parents that night.

Life in the 2000s became days filled with light because I got to India and started school.

When I was a shepherd on the mountains, the days were long, but days turned into minutes with the busy schedule of my boarding school life in India. I went to classes from 7:30 AM to 4:30 PM, and after school I had activities such as basketball, volleyball and knitting clubs.

\* \* \* \* \* \* \* \*

To keep from freezing, I wore hairy boots made from yak's skin and long skirts made out of sheep's skin. I also wore long-sleeved shirts and chupa—a Tibetan dress with a long skirt—handmade by my mom and grandma. On special occasions, I wore sneakers. In India, I wore regular dresslike T-shirts and pants and sneakers bought from the local Indian stores.

\* \* \* \* \* \* \* \*

My favorite memories of my life in Tibet are hearing the beautiful songs of the morning birds in the oak trees and feeling the warm, cozy hands of my grandma on my face, making me smile.

---

*Tashi Sangmo was born in Tibet and grew up in India and Brooklyn. She attended International High School in Brooklyn and Mount Holyoke College in South Hadley, Massachusetts.*

# The Secret

by MICHELLE SEUCAN, 2023

*A love letter to my summers in the Romanian countryside growing up. This story nostalgically reminisces about my adventures there, fusing elements of personal nonfiction with magical realism . . . a mini-memoir with a fantasy twist!*

In the middle of a Romanian nowhere, beyond the North star and past the Black Sea, lies a secret village.

Some may even view it as the Calypso's island of Eastern Europe, a quaint and elusive civilization that no one dares to enter. But if you look closely, maybe on an old tattered map from long ago, you'll see me there, spending every summer since birth with my family, raised by my grandparents and the adventurous potential of the village. It is here where I first learned to zoom down the rocky trails with my red, thrifted bicycle, waving to the tinkersmith who lived near the cemetery or the quiet, old woman by the church. To them, I was nothing more than a baby speck, but to me, they represented a mystery I couldn't quite wrap my head around.

I bonded with the village girls, learning their rhythm from midnight dances by the tinkersmith's abandoned house and exploring together the corn labyrinths that my grandfather always warned me never to explore. But being the curious little rebel that I am, I always followed the train of my thoughts, even if they led me down a path I might never come back from. I remember the mornings spent at Baraj Lake, picking wildflowers and chasing the ghosts of dandelions by wishing wells. We'd fall asleep in nearby meadows with daisies in our hair and crushed pears on our lips. And at night, after my grandmother's cheesecake dinners, I'd venture down yellow brick roads to the forbidden Atos Mountain, meeting them in abandoned houses or up white rose trees. Underneath the moon's Cheshire Cat smile, we'd softly share our dreams of life beyond the village. You see, I never knew what day it was or when it was time to go home, only summoned by my grandmother's distant voice when it was ora de lapte (milk hour). After all, time doesn't exist in Wonderland with your comrades.

While home was miles away in Staten Island suburbia, home was also in the middle of a Romanian nowhere with those village girls, forging friendships that you read about in fables or sonnets. It's strange how I've never seen them beyond the summer seasons—perhaps they're citizens of a dream world lightyears away. Whoever they may be, I'll forever remember them as my friends from beyond the North star and past the Black Sea.

Maybe we'll meet again in Wonderland.

*Michelle Seucan is a freshman at the University of North Carolina at Chapel Hill by way of New York City. Besides writing, she loves biking, going to museums, reading poetry, and traveling the world with family.*

## Tell Your Story

### A Prompt from Michelle Seucan

What cultural experiences or traditions from your upbringing were essential to your development and story as an individual? Write about them in a genre you don't usually write in (thriller, magical realism, comedy).

# Empire State

## by BRITTANY BARKER, 2010

Where I live, there is pride bellowing from the rooftops of rusted apartment buildings. Voices melted into the ground with choirs of mute prayers laid across city streets. This is nothing but home to me.

Sometimes I imagine myself a foreigner so I can see how she looks from the outside. I bet New York looks confused, with barbed-wire fences for teeth, a dancing skyline for a smile, and a shattered heart broken into five boroughs. I bet her tears flow like the Hudson River, her pride stands as tall as skyscrapers, and her personality is as playful as Riverbank State Park.

If I didn't know any better, I'd predict that she is an insomniac, a restless girl who never sleeps, with an "Empire State" of mind and theatrical feet.

A foreigner doesn't know the beauty of her insides like I do. New York is nothing but a home to me.

---

*Brittany Barker was born in Harlem, NY. She attended Hostos Lincoln Academy of Science in Bronx and Dickinson College in Carlisle, Pennsylvania.*

# Colorado
## by ASMA AL-MASYABI, 2023

*In this piece, I tried to look closely at what I love about the landscape that surrounds me everyday and discover what makes these familiar sights feel like home.*

*Asma Al-Masyabi is a poet, writer, visual artist, and creative writing student in Colorado. She enjoys whipping up chocolate chip cookies, buying new manga for her collection, and watching competitive cooking shows with her family.*

## Tell Your Story

### A Prompt from Asma Al-Masyabi

How would you describe your home city or state to someone who has never been there before? Think about the details, big and small, that stand out the most to you.

*This conversation is between current Publishing 360 mentee Asma Al-Masyabi and mentee alumni and poet Brittany Barker. Read Brittany's poem "Empire State" and read Asma's illustrated response, "Colorado," on page 92.*

**ASMA AL-MASYABI:** I really love your poetry. Can you tell me a little about yourself, how you came upon Girls Write Now, and what you do now?

**BRITTANY BARKER:** Thank you for choosing my poem. I wrote this in 2010, when I was a junior in high school and just getting my feet wet with poetry. It feels like a full circle moment to see this poem again when I haven't seen it in such a long time.

I stumbled upon Girls Write Now in around 2009 or 2010. My guidance counselor knew I was interested in poetry and writing and she was like, you should try out this program. I did the application process, and I started the following school year. It's been a beautiful experience. My time with Girls Write Now has really influenced who I am today.

Writing is very much a part of my life. Right now, I'm an Educational Consultant and a Creative Director for a company called Creative Soul House. I develop workshop experiences and programs for youth and adults and it merges the creative arts, social-emotional learning, and social justice. The creative element that I really got to explore in Girls Write Now is what lives inside of the way I teach and the way I show up for my own company. I just signed up for a poetry competition called the Women of the World Poetry Slam, and I'm getting back into a season where I want to make writing a primary thing in my life. That's where I currently am.

**AAM:** For me, Girls Write Now has really helped me bring writing to the forefront of my life. Before, I would do it on the side and mostly focus on school. But the program has really helped me to improve and focus on my writing.

You said you wrote your poem ten years ago. What did it feel like to re-read it after all this time? Did it remind you of some things you felt before?

**BB:** Yeah. It reminded me of the kind of writer I was at the time. It reminded me of my curiosity for my city. And it reminded me of those nights with my mentor, Joslyn, revising and then feeling the pressure of deadlines for the anthologies and so on.

I still believe that New York holds a lot of stories, some that are hidden and muted, some that have gotten to see the light of day. I still believe that there are a lot of places to play—to be yourself, to explore. And I still believe that to an outsider New York must look like this crazy confusing place. But once you find your spot in it, it's home.

**AAM:** That's a beautiful way of putting it. While I was reading the poem, I found it interesting that you talked about New York from an insider's perspective and that you also tried to look at it from an outsider's perspective. That was really neat, and something I really struggled with when writing my response. I had to walk around town and try to focus on what makes this place special to me. What might other people who visit pay attention to, that, for me, has kind of faded into the background?

**BB:** Right. Sometimes we can take where we're from for granted and it isn't until you go to a new place that you notice all the intricate small things. But then when you go home, it's like, that's just a building. That's just the sky.

I thought in your poem that you did that so beautifully. You talked about the hillsides and the rooftops and the sky with the cornfields and the snow. It made me curious about Colorado and it gave me an interesting visual for what it would look like. I've also been to Colorado, but I've never seen all those places that you described. You did a great job.

**AAM:** Thank you. For my poem, I tried to focus on the things I notice every day. You go out, you go to the grocery store, and in front of you, you see the mountains.

**BBM:** That's beautiful.

**AAM:** And there's Denver. I know, compared to New York, it's tiny.

**BB:** Do you live in Denver?

**AAM:** I live in Aurora, but I drive to Denver for college, and while you're driving you can see the skyline. It's pretty tiny, especially against the background of the mountains. I found it fun to play with perspective like that. Has your writing process changed since you wrote this poem?

**BB:** The writing process, yes. Most definitely. I would say back then I had a hard time letting go of lines. Sometimes I would think, this is a really good line, I want to keep it, I like the way it sounds. And my mentor would ask me, *but what purpose does it serve? Does it just sound nice or is it helping the reader see what you see?*

A lot of the time it was her trying to build that muscle memory in me. Now I would say it's definitely second nature to say very concisely what needs to be said. Of course, allow yourself time to move through the beauty—as you do wonderfully in your piece—but don't waste your words. Use each word wisely and if it's not needed, don't waste the reader's time. Sometimes less is more.

**AAM:** If you were to re-write this poem today, would you do anything differently?

**BB:** I would do a whole lot! I would definitely be more specific with the story. In the forest stanza, I talk about voices melted into the ground with choirs of mute prayers laid across city streets. I'm like, okay, that gives an image, but also, me now is like, what does that even mean? You can say that in so many ways. You can give some dialogue in this piece. You can say more about the city streets—what does a mute prayer look like across a city street? Does it tell the story of poverty? Does it tell the story of kids on the corner waiting to get a bacon egg and cheese from the store? What does it really look like? I would definitely show more, rather than tell.

**AAM:** They say a poem is never done. Looking back at my old poems, it's always hard not to want to change something about them.

**BB:** And a big question is, how do you know when your poem is done? That's my question for you. How did you know when "Colorado" was done?

**AAM:** Well, illustrating a poem is a bit different, because once you put the illustrations in you can't go in and change it. I had to think pretty hard on whether or not the text was where I wanted it to be. Since there are images involved, I tried to balance the words and the visuals. Sometimes the visuals support the words. For the text, I wrote it first and then I drew inspiration from your poem and what you focused on—the city streets, how she looks from the outside, barbed wire fence for teeth.

In mine, I said, "purple-jab compass felt into the horizon," so I focused on trying to mirror the elements of your poem. Then, once I was happy with where that was going, I had to then figure out if it sounded right. It took a few drafts. Then I tried to figure out how I wanted to portray it on the paper. Some of the images came to me more easily than the others. And you might notice that with the lines, one is zoomed in and the other is zoomed out, like looking at it from the inside versus the outside.

**BB:** Yes! That's creative. And you know something that you also did really well? You didn't use people to describe Colorado. You just used descriptions of the geography of Colorado to bring it to life. I really appreciated that. Even the last line, which reads "an asphalt laid . . . " You could have said people finding their way home, or leading to people's homes, but you said the streets and personified it. The streets are finding their way home. I thought that was just such a beautiful way to capture how alive Colorado is.

**AAM:** Thank you! That's actually something I take inspiration from you on. You described New York as a person. Like, you talked about *her*, and how the skyscrapers have personalities or how playful Riverbank State Park is. Although I didn't do that as directly, I still tried to have Colorado be the character.

**BB:** You did that very clearly.

**AAM:** Thank you. I know you're an educator. Could you tell me about why you chose that as a career path?

**BB:** Yeah. I'll start with a funny story. I think I was trying to be educated before I even knew I wanted to be an educator. Initially I thought I was going to be a neurologist and I had a very misinformed understanding of what neurology was. I was like, I like the way the brain works. Yeah, neurology. And then my counselor in high school told me I would have to take biology and I was like, yeah, no.

But the funny story is that when I was in third grade, I had a crush on this boy. We'll call him J. J and I used to make up these exams. I would print these tests and bring them to him at school. I was really excited and I was all for it, and one day he was like, why do you keep giving me all these tests? That experience is something I keep in mind. Because I didn't become an educator to test people. But there was just something bubbling there since I was very, very young.

I also really appreciated the spaces that a few of my teachers carved out for me. I went to an Early College school where professors come in and teach us things, and one of the courses was a Caribbean Literature course. And I had never seen myself in the classroom. I was learning about history, I was reading texts from authors who didn't look like me. And it wasn't until them that I noticed that my experience is worthy of study.

There are places and opportunities for you to feel affirmed in the classroom. Seeing that was sort of the heart of it. I wanted to replicate that experience for other people, because it was so integral to who I am and the way that I walk into a room, the way that I speak about myself, the way that I take care of my community. It's all because there were teachers who let me know that the experiences of people who look like me are worthy of study and a vital source of knowledge to help you move throughout this life.

I want to do that for other people and I want to make it fun. I want to be creative with it and I want people to know that learning and study don't have to be this boring, monotonous thing. You can learn through poetry, you can learn through exploring your emotions. That's the foundation of me wanting to be an educator.

**AAM:** That's such a beautiful reason. How does writing factor into your job as an educator?

**BB:** That's a great question. As I've grown and entered into my career, I've learned that everything is writing. Marketing, ads, billboards. Little old me in high school thought writing was just books and poetry, but it can live in so many places. Writing is alive in the curriculum I develop. I used to be an English teacher, so that's how I got started. I was writing about writing, about teaching, about language. That's how writing has lived.

I've done some playwriting classes. I've submitted a film to a film festival called Pursuit. And even though the words weren't on the screen, I was like, that's writing. You wrote that. Just consulting for companies and organizations, drafting a lesson plan, putting things together. Writing takes on so many different forms. Journaling. That's the flexibility of the craft. That's how it lives. I'm becoming more and more interested in the many different ways that I continue to try the skill in a new avenue or through a different lens.

**AAM:** Writing is applicable in so many different ways. What do you think draws you to poetry?

**BB:** I think I'm an introvert and that poetry is my honest space. It's a time for me to process and to imagine and be messy. I don't like to be messy in front of people. I like to be controlled and have my things together, but poetry is a space where I can come as myself. It exists between me and the page. I love it because I get the space to process, but I also get to imagine. I get to be the mess that I am in my head.

**AAM:** This is something I've had to do a lot. In creative writing classes they always ask, why poetry? I think what I like about it is what you were talking about, the cutting away. I feel like it's language with everything extra cutaway, and you can really get to the heart of what you're trying to explain. It's that one-on-one connection with you and a poem where you're not trying to hide anything.

**BB:** I love that. The power of poetry is that you can start it in one place, and then in three minutes—if we're talking about performance—you can take your listener somewhere else. Poetry gets you right at the heart of the thing to make you feel. It can make you change the way you think. The shifting is really beautiful.

# Identity
## BY PRISCILLA GUO, 2013

*An ode to being seen and heard in all my multitudes.*

Like the epidermis, papillary, reticular layers,
and the subcutaneous tissue,
that make up my skin
And most people can't get past that
the layers they can see.
But the other parts
they're still part of me.
You want to take one part, two parts,
But take me as a whole.
You've got to listen, listen real close
to hear for my soul.
When you see me,
you pigeonhole.
You put me in one role.
Ethnicity: Asian.
Slick black hair and a name
that rhymes with Ping
Really good at math,
a cold unblinking thing.
When you hear me,
don't hear Asian.
I am layered
And that means I'm intricate.
Don't read that like I'm delicate
Gender: Yes, female.
And I've heard it all
But I'm your equal
so, don't call me doll
When you hear me,
don't hear Woman.
I'm layered
And that means I am an enigma.
Take me as I am

Not how you perceive me.
Age: 16
And that don't mean a thing.
I can be wise, immature,
But my voice,
that's what endures.
When you hear me,
don't hear teenager.
I'm layered
And that means I am immeasurable even by
years.
Don't dissect me
like one of your experiments in high school.
Here's the right ventricle.
There's the hypothalamus.
Here's where you listen and
here's where you stop.
That's not how my voice works.
And when you hear me,
I want you to hear my voice
Better yet, listen to my voice.
Drink up my voice.
Live my voice.
That can flow like sweet honey or
sting with bitter rinds.
I am layered.
Peel back the layers and peel back.
You'll find my voice
just like it was hiding in the back of your closet
or underneath your chair.
It dances along forever between these parts,
because I am layered.

---

*Priscilla Guo is a Girls Write Now mentee alum who is passionate about advocating for justice at the intersection of civil rights and technology. She is pursuing a J.D. at Stanford Law School and holds degrees from Tsinghua, Oxford, and Harvard.*

# Layers Unseen

## BY DOM DAWES, 2023

*[Multidimensionality] obfuscates historical origins// and lights paths to internal awakenings.*

Said people will not get past
knowing what constructs
our layered skin.
They strive to imitate the layers,
while demonizing its original owners.
To them, the multidimensionality
of our epidermis, papillary, reticular layers—
Obfuscates their historical origins,
while they rip apart
the racial separateness they created.
But to us, it lights paths to internal awakenings.
It shields us
from their blaring gaze.
You put me in one role.
Race: Black.
Thick 'unruly' hair and unlawfulness
that leads to cells, coffins, and penury.
Really good at selling sex with plump assets,
can make some collard greens?
When you hear me,
don't hear African American.
I am layered
And that means I'm pyramidal
Please read me as delicate
Gender: Anything but female.
Yet that's all I hear.
But I'm your equal
so, don't call me baby

When you hear me,
Don't hear Woman.
I am transdimensional
That simply listening will explain.
Take me as whatever you experience first—
My blackness, queerness, or both.
Age: 19
Surprised I made it.
I too can be wise, immature,
But my voice,
that has been passed down.
When you hear me,
don't hear African American.
I'm layered
And that means I am immeasurable even by
unquantifiable experiences.
Dissect weapons used against me,
and my identities.
Here's the liver's hepatic duct.
There's the diaphragm.
Here's where you listen using findings to
reflect.
That's how our voices work.
And when you hear us,
you will hear pleas and war cries
Better yet, you will listen to our voices.
Soak in our harmonies.
Live all of our pitches.
That can flow like sweet coconut water or
sting with bitter polyphenol.
I am layered.
Gently peel back the layers.
You'll find our voices
just like they were singing dramatic opera

in a soundproofed space.

It bounces forever between these parts,

because we are layered.

---

*Dom Dawes (he/they) is a sophomore at Hunter College. With the help of his four-legged black alarm clock, he majors in English Literature with a concentration in creative writing and minors in Jewish Studies.*

## Tell Your Story

### A Prompt from Dom Dawes

Whether to the public, oneself, or both, everyone has their share of unseen layers. These layers deserve to be addressed by their names and recognized for their impact—and that's where you come in. Using an art form of your choosing, discuss your experience with hidden layers. How did you and/or others perceive these layers? And upon realizing this, what was your reaction? Did anything change?

# A Touch of Memory Between Amsterdam and a Guy Named Columbus

## BY JASMINE HOLLOWAY, 2008

*They say New York City has millions of different people with millions of different versions of the City itself. Here is mine…*

We set our scene at 125 West 109th Street, between Columbus and Amsterdam—my home. I have lived here all my life, a few blocks from Nancy, but this neighborhood holds different memories for me. I remember waiting in my building's lobby on a cold winter's day for the small yellow bus to arrive and pick up my brother for school. The number "12" painted on the left side of the lobby door in brown and the number "5" painted on the right. I always wondered if "5" was ever lonely there underneath the dim, shaded light. I remember riding my new pink and white tricycle in the outside yard of my building, one story above ground and the regular dirty streets of Amsterdam. In between the dark brown trees that hovered over my small body, I tried to avoid every crack and misplaced rock on the ground. Yet still, I would fall. I never rode that bike again. I remember walking down the narrow hallways of my home in 8B and the cold sensation of my two little chubby feet touching the smooth tiles on the floor. I remember moving into 11H, a new apartment much bigger than the last. Three rooms instead of two. The distance between my family and me wasn't apparent at the time as the warmth of my new home wrapped around my body like a warm blanket. I knew this was forever. Tender years came and went. I blindly sat by thinking these four walls and everything they hold are immortal. Nothing damaged, nothing lost, just kept together.

That was until materialistic dreams turned into concrete reality, crashing down on top of my head like heavy rain. Moving again, 10K gave each of us our own space, dividing my family members one by one, making the space that existed between us larger. It tugged at the strings of my adolescent heart to leave my worn-out church dresses in the vacant closets of the house that wasn't my home anymore. It was the place where the rest of my estranged family broke their last bread together, before their once intertwined paths in life crossed no more.

Now, I have removed my still-framed life and joined the fast-paced world, *outside* of the walls that cocooned me. I brush my chubby ebony fingers along the cold, rusty black bars of a vacant lot owned by Con Edison next to my building. The wind creeps up on me as I pass the old weathered signs saying, "Bush lies, who dies" or "Need a house maid?"

I stand at the corner and see the dark, gloomy Cathedral, the old newspapers whirling like a tornado on the ground, leaves blowing across my feet. Home isn't far from here... from here, it's never too far.

---

*Jasmine Holloway (she/her) is a former mentee of Girls Write Now. Jasmine now works at a Brooklyn school and teaches theatre on the side. She would like to thank Nancy for mentoring her all those years ago.*

# Dear Mia

## BY MIA DOWDELL, 2023

*This piece centers on a love for writing and
a life-changing third-grade teacher.*

We set our scene on Hammond Street in Los Angeles, where I went to school. Entering my third grade classroom felt like stepping into the paper dome of a sunlit lamp. Its oculus—three wide windows—filtered light through glittering paper fish on a clothesline above our heads. As I sat cross-legged on the rainbow carpet, Mrs. Melzer painted a world of Roald Dahl giants and a type of magic that pillowed the sky. It was on this rainbow carpet that I imagined the thread sticking out from the hem of my polo. A worm unhooked itself from the earth, separated from its colony. I gently tugged it out and released it onto the floor.

Months went by and soon I was trick-or-treating with friends in their gated community. The neighborhood was much wealthier than the one I grew up in, only thirty minutes away. Houses were sliced into rows of pastel cakes down the street and yards painted in pistachio hues. My tiny thumb pressed titanium doorbells all night. Each time, I wondered if it would fail to make an electronic chime. A castle with no voice. Trick or treat! As the door opened, I looked around for low ceilings and rugged carpets, just like my house had on the other side of town. But none were to be found.

The asphalt track at school transformed into a riot of black and blue glitter at the Halloween parade the next day. The sun beamed down and the thin frills on my handmade witch's skirt fried against my metal seat. Our class sat in rows and waited for our turn to showcase our costumes to our friends and family. I counted plastic tiaras, hoop skirts and other costumes I had seen before inside Party City catalogs that came in the mail but I couldn't afford. When my little sister dressed as Belle wandered away from her group, I found her in the crowd and invited her to sit with me and my classmates.

"You're such a great big sister, Mia!" Mrs. Melzer beamed. "You remind me of me and my sister, always looking out for each other." In a crowd of monsters, I felt braver than ever.

In January, Mrs. Melzer introduced a new project: a pen pal short story exchange between my class and other third graders across Connecticut. Without a second thought, my wrist skated across the page forming bubblegum spirals enveloped within a great quilt of language that I hoped would lift someone up into the sky. I thought of how my mother made her jewelry. She'd press and fold and weave and twist for hours, wordless and tunnel-visioned like a ritual was being performed before me and the slightest sound I made could disturb the spirits. Just as weaving was a sport that belonged to my mother, writing was becoming something of mine. My story was a transit map. Each punctuation mark darted towards a new destination to secret locations reserved only for my stranger. Mrs. Melzer tapped me on the shoulder. She read it, and smiled. "I wish more students cared about their work the way you do. I love this," she said. I got my letter back two weeks later. A single word, "sorry," was printed in a small font size near the top of the page. Mrs. Meltzer knew what she was talking about. When it comes to writing, some students don't care. For me, not only did I care, very much in fact, but it didn't feel like work and I liked that. My teacher's kind words tugged the threads of embarrassment back into place. Her encouragement caused my cheeks to burn. But it was the expression on her face that day when she quietly read the piece to herself in the corner of the classroom that reappears to me when I doubt my own voice.

On the last day of third grade, I looked around for my favorite teacher. My dad had been offered a job in San Francisco and we were preparing to move upstate. I found Mrs. Melzer in the hall to say goodbye. After I told her the news, she adjusted her square-shaped glasses and furrowed her brow, but then said she needed to leave soon for a teacher's meeting. With what little time I had, I tried to step beyond my introversion and thank her for everything she'd done for me, but I couldn't find the words. I left school that day disappointed. If I had anything at all, it was supposed to be language.

A few months later, I received a letter at our new home in San Francisco. It was from Mrs. Melzer! I tore it open and read it aloud. "Dear Mia, I hope you're doing well at your new school. Remember to keep going. I know you'll do spectacular things." Her words felt as though she was bringing me in for a hug right in my living room, protecting me with her gingerbread warmth. Her words, forever immortalized, live now in the top drawer of my desk.

*Mia Dowdell (she/her) is a high school senior with a love for poetry and matcha-flavored anything. She will attend UCLA majoring in English in the fall.*

## Tell Your Story

### A Prompt from Mia Dowdell

Write a story solely by describing a space or setting in detail that symbolizes a complicated feeling. What characteristics of the space contrast or are related to one another to represent this feeling?

# TTYL
## BY SARAI ARROYO, 2012

*Retrospectively, I did not like my story until Julia pulled it out of
the woodwork and reminded me why I told it in the first place: to
never forsake the facets that made me.*

Tom remembered perfectly his first encounter with a city girl, and with her
father, at age seven. Every detail, meaningless and important, had to be remembered as though one day it would save his life. Besides, how could any
boy forget a time when his mother forced him into a wool suit for his aunt's
outdoor wedding on one of the hottest days in the history of Georgia?

He was sweating bullets that day, no joke. The sun was high in the sky
and the taunting table of drinks a few feet from his reach wasn't helping.
Just as he was about to fake a stomach cramp, a tornado flew past him and
towards a wealthy-looking couple. Tom remembered the girl's butter-yellow
curls that stopped at the center of her back. The thickly lashed brown eyes
that fluttered to her shoes whenever making contact with his. It was the first
time something had held his attention span longer than the giant cake in his
view.

At first it seemed as though there was no chance of them making verbal
contact with each other. Her parents carried her around like a new trophy,
flashing her fancy white dress to every envious middle-class couple holding
their plainly dressed child. When the adults realized that the vast number of
children present would disturb the ceremony, they sent them to play tag and
seek before the priest's arrival. Tom watched the girl beg her skeptical parents
to let her go, her trembling lips threatening to wail loudly. They gave in and
ushered her away. Tom followed after her.

He immediately ducked behind the widest oak tree he spotted, holding
in his giggles as he watched several pairs of legs collapse to the ground dra-
matically being tagged. The slow search for hiders began to lull Tom into a
semi-conscious state. He settled himself into the soft grass, certain no one
would find him, until a soft voice whispered into his ear, "Can I hide with
you?"

His eyes sprang open and all he saw was white intertwined with yellow hair. "Uh, sure."

Tag and seek had lost its fun in less than ten minutes so it was only natural that fist-fights began over who got to go on the swing-sets first. But Tom and Courtney remained behind the tree, engrossed in learning about each other.

He was your typical farm boy, feeding chickens, riding horses, and then retiring to his hammock. She was from Atlanta, living in a nice condo with two attorney parents. They attended the wedding because her father had won a case for Tom's aunt and couldn't pass up a chance to see cleaned-up farmers in holy matrimony. Speak of the devil.

"*Courtney!* Where have you been? The kids were allowed back fifteen minutes ago!"

Up close, the man looked every bit as powerful and important as Tom assumed when he saw him from a distance; from the well-oiled hair to his shiny oxfords. His aunt would've called him "the man of my dreams" if she hadn't already gotten married—and if his face wasn't sneering. Poor Tom felt himself fuse with the dirt as those dark eyes continued to stare him down.

"Daddy, I'm okay, I'm just talking to Tom—"

"Well enough of that, besides, I told you many times that you are not allowed to be alone with *boys*."

"But—"

"We're leaving. Now."

The adamant expression on Courtney's face did not falter as she stood up slowly and walked to her father's side. Tom felt a hundred protesters well up in his throat but he held them back: What was he to say? *Please let your daughter stay here in the countryside and be my friend?*

She looked at Tom again and said, "TTYL."

And just like that his heart deflated like a balloon.

Courtney and her father walked away, hand in hand, walking ten years into the future where Courtney's father lost his job (and wife) for favoring alcohol and snide remarks. They would move to the countryside to avoid further humiliation where Courtney would finish her senior year in Jameson High School and reunite with Tom after accidently spilling soda on his pants before identifying him. He recognized her, though.

After stopping her mid-apology and giving her his name, he smiled at the light of recognition in her eyes, gestured to his pants and said, "TTYL."

---

*Sarai Arroyo is a Girls Write Now alumni, circumstantial workaholic, and eternally bookish thrill seeker who'll coax a laugh out of anyone just because it tugs at her heartstrings.*

# Swap
## BY JULIA ANDRESAKIS, 2023

*Two high schoolers in creative ruts meet in a forest.*

This was what it was all about, Clara thought as her fingers hovered along the keyboard with the delicacy of a pianist before a showcase. Doing the writing thing, putting graphite to woodpulp—or black digits to a white screen, whatever. It was tough, but, boy, when the words flowed, they were good: they hit all the resonant notes, their cadence made for being perfectly read aloud or in one's mind, and she felt like she had truly captured some precious, finite essence of life that could only be lived through her prose. If only this momentum lasted for more than two well-crafted sentences at a time, divine little geysers gushing in a desert before leaving her page a wasteland. *It's a problem of discipline, not motivation,* her mother rang in her ears. *You're too talented to be this lazy. Lazy girls do not get college scholarships.*

*It's nothing to do with laziness, Mother,* Clara retorted in her head. *It's about letting the passion fuel me.* Still: her drive hadn't done her many favors in the hour she'd been sitting at the big oak desk, so perhaps her mother was onto something. She positioned herself in front of the window, where the trees were nearly every shade between green and red, swaying from a continual breeze, the weight of birds nesting and taking flight on and off their branches. The thrum of the Hudson. A month since she'd been uprooted from the city and the natural beauty of the world still threw her into a state of disbelief.

So far she had some fragments: *Ethereal trees. Birdsongs I wish I knew the lyrics to. The river speaks clearer to those who approach with kindness and curiosity.* Then, in a fit of frustration, she wrote: *WHAT DOES ANY OF THAT EVEN MEAN?!?!?* before wiping the document bare. She closed the laptop, rubbed the bridge of her nose, and reasoned it was time for field notes—observations about life around her recorded in her trusty notepad. She slipped on her sneakers and set off into the woods. Every few steps she paused to write something down: *Auburn leaf falls from tallest tree. Saw a very fat or very pregnant squirrel.*

About a mile down the way, as she approached the river and the sun began to rise through the clouds, she saw a hooded figure hunched over on a stump. She scrawled down: Mustard yellow hoodie. *Hood not completely covering head, left side tucked behind an ear. Slouched like a parenthesis on a diagonal.*

The figure shot up like a spooked deer and turned her way just long enough for her to notice his thick lenses, disheveled dark curls, and pock-marked cheeks. He squinted, then returned to his hunched position. Moving a few steps closer toward the river and the stump, Clara saw that he was balancing a sketchpad on his lap, a pack of pastel-colored pencils in a bed of leaves beside him.

"You an artist?" she said.

"Trying," he replied without looking up. He tore a page of his pad and stuffed it in his pocket. He began another outline. "I can't get the contour of the stream right."

Clara nodded as though she got what he meant. "I get what you mean," she said. "Looks like a tricky... curve."

"What are you scribbling in your notebook?" he asked, eyes still fixed on the landscape.

"Observations." At his silence, she added, "I'm a writer. A struggling one, but still."

"Ah, I draw because I can't write for squat."

"I write because I've got the motor skills of a preschooler."

He laughed with an exhale of air through his nose, looked back down at his pad, and tore the page. "Humiliating how hard this is for me."

"Let's swap," said Clara. "You write about this scene in front of you for twenty minutes. I'll draw it."

Considering the proposal, the boy pushed his glasses up and let his hood fall down. He shifted to make room on the stump and Clara sat down. Without ceremony, they traded materials. At the end, they switched back, each delighted by the other's creation. He liked how cartoonish Clara's landscape was; Clara appreciated the clarity and simplicity of his sentences, their sheer lack of pretentiousness. It reminded her how loose and free writing could be.

"All artists sign their names," he said. So she did. She handed her note-pad back to him, asking for the same. Elliot, he wrote.

Sometimes, over the following years, she supposed he was an apparition; he became the inspiration for her regional award-winning story, "Ghost in the Woods." Still, she returned often to that spot down the road from her house, hoping to see the hunched artist once more. To no avail.

Her senior year of college, many states away, Clara sat cross-legged in the patch of campus grass overlooking the koi pond. She opened her laptop and typed gingerly into a document called "Final Manuscript." When she hit a lull, she closed the machine, stared into the water. Then she felt a shadow envelop her.

She looked up and saw a bespeckled, hooded boy holding out his tablet. "Let's swap?"

---

*Julia Andresakis is a writer from Brooklyn. She enjoys wandering, Midwest emo music, and dolls with haunted auras. In a past life, she was probably a court jester.*

## Tell Your Story

### A Prompt from Julia Andresakis

Think of a word or phrase you associate with a specific person. What is the origin of that association? Write a scene in which the phrase plays a significant role in two characters' communication.

# Tell Your Story
## A Prompt from Zaina Arafat

Continue this prompt: "I am both…"

In doing so, think of a contradiction that exists within you. For example: I am both extroverted and introverted, I am both messy and clean, I am "both" American and Arab.

Show us how you embody that contradiction, what being "both" looks like for you. Allow us to see you in a moment where we can see both of those aspects at play.

---

*Zaina Arafat is a Palestinian-American writer and the author of the novel,* You Exist Too Much. *Her stories and essays have appeared in publications including* Granta, The New York Times, The Believer, Virginia Quarterly Review, *VICE,* BuzzFeed, The Atlantic *and* NPR. *She holds an MA in international affairs from Columbia University and an MFA from the University of Iowa and is a recipient of the Arab Women/ Migrants from the Middle East fellowship at Jack Jones Literary Arts. She grew up between the United States and the Middle East and currently lives in Brooklyn.*

*People say, "Are you a poet now? Are you an essayist now?" and I'm like, "No, I'm just a writer." I think, as a writer, we get to write, and we get to do whatever you feel like in that moment is the right kind of writing for you. I really do look at myself as a storyteller, both of fiction stories as well as nonfiction stories.*

— DARIEN HSU GEE, Girls Write Now Teaching Artist and Author of *Allegiance*

# Stunned Silence

## BY WINKIE MA, 2015

*CW: mentions of sexual violence*

*This piece speaks to the loud thoughts and unspoken truths of being a girl in New York.*

I had been walking for thirty minutes, yet I still couldn't figure out if I was cold from the March breeze biting at my cheeks that Sunday morning, or from the chill tickling my spine. I kept my head down, staring at the splatters of blackened gum on the pavement. I had to step carefully around shattered Heineken bottles and I was only an inch away from stomping on a fresh glob of spit.

Silence.

I glanced up, seeing colossal brick buildings, all red and identical. I decided I could go to one of the convenience shops around me until I felt safe to walk again. To my dismay, all their windows were plastered with FOR RENT signs. Bright purple and orange graffiti littered their metal shutters. I tightened my jaw, unable to shake off the eerie sensation.

*You're almost at Janet's house,* I reminded myself, *if there are even houses there . . .*

All the neighborhoods I had known had smiling people and colorfully chalked sidewalks, but never had I been in such a desolate place. I hoped that it was 57th Street already, where she lived. Soon I would be there, and soon we would be finished with the art project, and soon I would be out of this neighborhood for good. But it was only 63rd Street, and I silently reprimanded myself for not taking another route.

My panic worsened when I caught sight of four men one long block ahead. They stood in front of a giant shutter. Though their voices were muffled, I could make out cusses directed at the few people who passed by, and even at such a distance, the smoke from their cigarettes was repulsive. Fright pervaded my senses. My eyes widened. Anxiously, I looked to see if I could go elsewhere, but the opposite sidewalk was closed off. This was the only place to walk through.

*Maybe Janet can come pick me up.*

*Keep cool.*

*They're gonna kill me.*

*They're harmless!*

As I approached, I strayed right by the curb in hopes of going unnoticed. My mother had always warned me to stay away from these types of men, but I reassured myself that they had the morality not to bother me. I loosened up even more after realizing that all the people they'd harassed were adults. *I'm 14*, I thought. *I'm a minor. They won't do anything.*

But when I looked up, the man on the right already had his gaze set on me.

He took a puff from his cigarette and smirked, eyes trailing from the top of my beanie to the bottom of my boots. "Hey, you goin' anywhere?" The man next to him followed suit. "Yeah, mami, need a little help?" he hollered in a raspy voice.

My pace quickened. As I walked briskly past them, I tried to block their raucous laughter out. I hid my face deeper into my scarf in an attempt to become invisible, though it was no use. I already felt completely exposed. The men could see right through me, could smell the dripping fear. I was so uneasy that their continuous taunts became white noise in my ears.

My heart had a thundering pound. I turned around at the next block, relieved to see that they hadn't followed me. They were just blurred figures in the background, smoking and waiting for another person to shout at. After a while, they were out of sight.

I teetered down the pavement. Any thought of the art project had vanished. Instead, my mind was flooded with the sound of their heavy voices. I shivered when I thought of their ravenous eyes scanning my body and pulled my jacket closer to my chest. I glanced behind me again and again, and once more for good measure to make sure they weren't following me.

All of a sudden, the fear became fury. My fingernails dug deeper into my palms with every angry thought. I was disgusted at what they did. I was furious that I gave off such a vulnerable impression. Would anything have changed if I stood up for myself instead? Would I feel better now?

In my head, I created a different scenario. I pictured myself with my chin tilted upward and my shoulder blades pressed against each other. I pictured myself standing as tall as a 5 foot girl could go. I pictured myself telling each and every one of them: "Go to hell!"

But all that had come out was stunned silence.

---

*Winkie Ma (she/her) was a mentee at Girls Write Now from 2014 to 2017. She attended Emory University for her undergraduate studies and is now pursuing a PhD in psychology.*

# Echoing Strength

## BY CATHY SHENG, 2023

*CW: mentions of sexual violence*

*This piece is about fears and growth. It's about wounds and healing.*
*It's a story about a girl's journey from silence to strength,*
*and breaking the molds society has cast for girls.*

I leaned into the shadow, gripping the rough, paint-splattered brick wall as I caught my breath. My thoughts pounded slowly as if trying to connect with the next thought through sludge; disorientation made the pounding worse. My hands ran continuously up and down my arms in desperation, rubbing off the distasteful stares and the dirt of their words.

Drip. Drip. Drip. My hand reached up and came away wet and trembling. Tears ran down the defeating slants of my cheeks and bruised my collars a deep green. Yet silence still swallowed me in its suffocating hold. I felt diaphanous and unanchored, poked and prodded everyday with stares that snagged too long in places unwanted, with abrupt car rides at the deli store, with possessive touches at my neck, my arm, my hair—invading my space and mind. I became a floating figure darting from streetlight to streetlight. I didn't know by simply walking I was inviting harassment.

Suddenly overcome with rage, I gritted the gravel beneath my feet and viciously kicked. Guiltily satisfied, I continued aiming my indignation and still-lit fury of the world's injustices toward it.

Exhausted, I stopped kicking and closed my eyes. I was immediately awash with a sense of helplessness. Eyes closed, I slid down the gritty wall, legs tangled in jaunty-angled branches, hands covering my eyes though they were closed already. I wondered how many women have been rooted in that same position. The wind blowing putrid air toward their faces. Somewhere to be, someone to be, yet stuck in this endless in between. Stuck in a god-forbidden alleway in who-knows-which street. Abandoned and alone, shameful of a wrong that others inflicted, indignant yet stifled with silence.

In the distance, I still hear their hooting screeches of laughter and smell the sharp cigarette smoke wafting in from the wind. But they were fading in and out, each time growing louder. Louder, as if drawing closer.

Then there was a beat of silence. Light shuffling on concrete that broke the pattern. I frowned, ears perked.

A sharp, female gasp rose, then cut off in the air. Another unfortunate soul who took the wrong turn in the streets. My nerves grew taut, and my stomach knotted.

An appreciative, low growl greeted her. Bile rose in my throat. I crept around the edge, half-in and half-out of the shadow peering at the unfolding scene. Somebody even had the audacity to hoot, and I could imagine with a pooling dark loathing the body-scanning gaze that followed.

"Even prettier than the other hun that came aroun.' Wouldn't you say so?" drawled the one with the raspy voice.

Eagerly, the other's grating voice answered "Right-o. You make quite the pair . . . though I can't see you all that well standin' all alone there." With searching eyes and a hungry smile, "Why don't you come on over?" The other mimed touching her, his roving hands massaging the air.

The girl's shoulder quaked, and she rocked on her heels. I gripped my hands in a white-knuckled grasp, screaming internally for her to turn on her heels and walk and walk and never turn back.

With an impatient toss of his head, the cigarette man with several piercings dangling across his left brow and a balded back side crisscrossed with scars, threw down his cigarette. It flew down in a flutter of sparks; in one sharp movement he mushed it into a pulp.

Then, as if moving with one mind, both of them inched closer, hands shoved into their pockets, only their teeth gleaming in the dimming light. The girl blinked long and hard, coming out of her stupor. She flung her phone out—the screen, a blaring light against the dark canvas of the evening. Her fingers started moving with anxious wildness.

"Hmm . . . a rebellious one aren't you?" He stepped even closer, an arm's length away, her hands fluttered uselessly by her side. "Lucky for you I've got some time."

She stood there in stunned silence.

Their hands came up and shot forward, aiming for her phone.

Without thinking, I marched out of the shadows, fury etched into every feature, powering my strides to be longer and defiant.

I have no idea what I am doing.

No. I do know.

Because this silence, this silence has saved no one, and I need to break through it. Too long silence has branded me, made me cower in my shoes, made me shadow my eyes and shame my existence, made me disguise my face and body in smothering darkness, made me submit to them under their silver smiles, double-edged words, and probing touches.

I've had enough.

"Put your hands down," I asserted through clenched teeth, whether because of anger or fear I don't know. I tossed a swift look at the girl. Her eyes were still wide as saucers but they gleamed with a defiance that wasn't there before. She nodded solemnly.

"Oh my, is that not the stunnin' gal that came by before? Why look, she couldn't leave for long," he said unbothered, laughing as if it's all a greatly orchestrated joke. Their faces were twisted into sneers; we weren't the first people to have walked here. They were used to this power, this submission; they fed and grew dominance from it. What's a little word, just a bit of silly pettiness that would be over quickly.

I continued willing steel into my voice knowing the fight was long from over, "You think you can just prowl around and stroke our arms, eat us up with your dirty stares like we are museum displays," I exclaimed, tears threatening to spill. But I will not, I will not be vulnerable, I will not open another wound for them to sink into and break down.

"We are just normal human beings like you. We are just walking around, doing nothing wrong, and yet we instantly become targets. Our eyes are trained on any eyes that stay a second too long, on every movement in case it was a lurking somebody, doubting every person no matter their good intentions. This is the world we live in. We are criminals in our own body," I continued, hands made into fists.

"Where and why do you feel this right?" the girl said, "Do you ever feel a trace of guilt, of shame? We feel invaded, petrified, and demeaned every living second on the street because of you, yet you do it as if for pleasure." Something changed in her. Demeanor no longer frail, the girl stood with authority.

"When has this become acceptable? When?" I cried indignantly, my years of stored rage rising to the surface, my voice clanging for the chance we long deserved. "If you dare step foot on this block, if you dare touch a single hair on us, if you dare. You'll find yourself a step away from prison," I whispered, low and dangerous, but enough to be carried by the wind.

One was frozen in mid-raise of his hand, his jaws dropped low and slack, no doubt hearing these words for the first time in his life. Would have been comical, if not for the incident. The other rubbed the bald side of his head, staring bullets at us, but he was already hurriedly moving in the opposite direction.

Then I turned on my heels and walked, filling my steps with confidence, my jacket billowing around me, carefree, my hair a symphony of directions. I nodded at the girl. She looked mildly stunned, frozen features that were still comprehending the madness of the past hour. Suddenly, her face split into a grin, then a great howl.

I smiled in return. I smiled at having triumphed over my greatest fear, of finally, finally, owning my space, my voice. I have done it. We have done it. We are warriors; we deserve to laugh on the streets, to walk on the streets with no fear. To shatter this stunned silence that's captured so many women, with echoing strength.

Turning onto 57th street, I was filled with conviction. I knew precisely what I was going to do for the art project. It's due time for the brush strokes to paint a different message.

With echoing strength, I repeated.

---

*Cathy Sheng (she/her) lives in sunny California, and loves a good read and getting lost in fictitious worlds. In her free time she enjoys delving into thought-provoking sci-fi, getting lost in doodling, or playing a Debussy piece.*

## Tell Your Story

### A Prompt from Cathy Sheng

Write about a meeting between you and the past you, about a fear, grudge, or hatred that you've eventually outgrown or overcome. What advice would you give? How would you react? Write it as a play.

# Skinny Girl Memoir
## BY NATALIE MOJICA, 2017

*Growing up surrounded by women of color, I always felt isolated by the fact that my body was different than those of the beautiful women around me. This poem was my moment of solidarity; my body is no one's but my own and I don't need anyone else's approval.*

I know distance more than I know company,
and when my family pinches at the fat around my
waist I am taken back to the motherland for a
brief moment. my grandmother is sitting in the
backyard, drinking the cafe bustelo my mother
sent her and smiling, she beckons me towards her
and I set on her lap blissful and naive to what the
next twelve years of my life will become. the moment
ends almost as quickly as it started and my aunt is
questioning if I eat enough at home, my cousin is
grimacing as her curves are compared to the angles
my body is made out of and both of our bodies
have become spilled coffee stains on the floor for
other people to step on; everyone in my aunt's
too small kitchen is laughing and I feel as if somebody
has set me on fire. my skin becomes paper
and my skeleton becomes full of the debris I tried
so desperately to sweep under the rug my twelve-year-old insecurities
come flying out again like a genie
from a magic lamp simply by the sound of drunken
family laughter and I cannot breathe. I have never
smoked before but in that moment I swear there is not
oxygen in the world and my lungs are filled with
tobacco made from the scars on my body that never
healed and nicotine-like unspilled tears. my cousin is
blushing and I know that it bothers her that her father's
friend is staring at her in a way less than appropriate because

it bothers me that my father's friend is staring at me as
if I were a blow-up doll made simply for his pleasure.
the twelve year old inside of me, filled with insecurities is
screaming with shame but the fourteen-year-old me is
sighing because she knows—
we've been through this process so many times we
know it by heart, it is wrong but it is to be expected and
the newly fifteen-year-old girl I have become stays silent.
I pretend that my aunt's sharp fingernails poking me
don't feel like knives, I smile and laugh with them,
when my aunt says that my hips are finally growing in
I do not say that this is not an accomplishment, that
my body growing is not a trophy for the public to stare
at. instead I nod and feel my throat constrict with
anger so immense it is like a monsoon inside of me. but
I do not speak. my obedience has become a habit too
hard to break. I know distance more than I know
company because even if my body is an abandoned home
that grows only weeds in the backyard it is my
abandoned home.

*Natalie Mojica is a Girls Write Now Mentee Alum, Class of 2019.*

# enough
## BY MAHDIA TULLY CARR, 2023

*This piece is about the societal pressures put on young women and girls to appear attractive by society's standards.*

If to you I am not good enough

but to them I am the standard,

if to them I am too dark to be pretty

but to you I am beautiful.

If I cannot fit inside the boxes that

everyone tells me I have to fit

in, then am I nothing after all?

It's unfair that being exactly who I am, how

I was born

isn't enough. I have to

hide behind ideals I can never reach

to be the person the rest of the world wants.

But the world is indecisive, and

I can never be what everyone wants.

I can never be good enough.

When will me be good enough for

everyone

and not just me?

When can I stop changing myself and my body,

when can the body I was born with be

good enough for the world.

If I like it, it should be okay.

But it's not,

and I'm

not.

---

*Mahdia Tully Carr (she/her) is a seventeen-year-old junior in high school, who is an avid writer, singer, and thinker.*

## Tell Your Story

### A Prompt from Mahdia Tully Carr

In your opinion, how do society's standards impact people's perceptions of themselves?

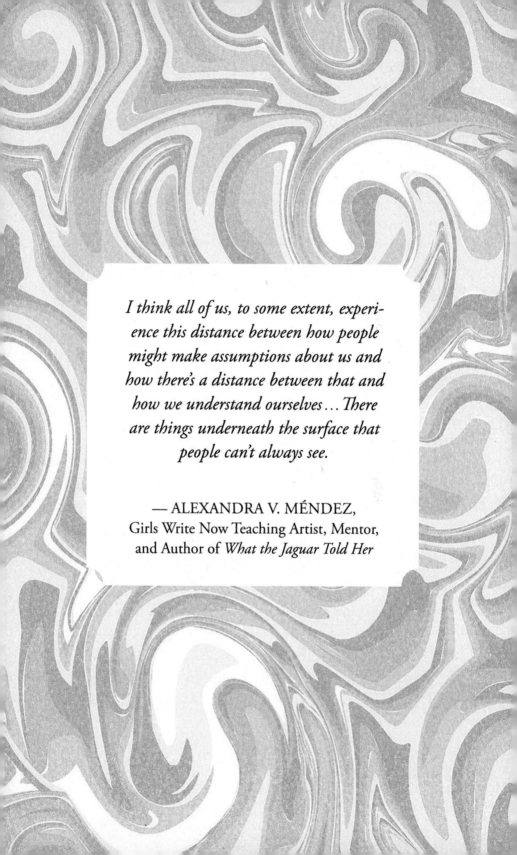

*I think all of us, to some extent, experi-
ence this distance between how people
might make assumptions about us and
how there's a distance between that and
how we understand ourselves . . . There
are things underneath the surface that
people can't always see.*

— ALEXANDRA V. MÉNDEZ,
Girls Write Now Teaching Artist, Mentor,
and Author of *What the Jaguar Told Her*

# WRITING
# AND
# PUBLISHING
# TIPS

# WRITING TIPS

*Writing can be a lonely, solitary experience. How can I best involve others in my writing practice?*

"I think for writers, in order to maintain your creativity, you have to be engaged. Even though writing is a solitary type of activity, you still have to be engaged in the world because that's where your inspiration comes from."

— DONNA HILL, Girls Write Now Mentor Alum and author of *After the Lights Go Down* and *Confessions in B-Flat*

"Find two to three people you trust, whose reading taste you respect, to read your work and give you honest feedback. When you've been working on something in your silo, it's so helpful to have someone who isn't as close to the work give you their perspective. It also opens up the opportunity to further engage with them. If someone has read your two-or three-hundred page draft, they are invested in seeing you complete the best version possible."

— NANA BREW-HAMMOND, Girls Write Now Mentor Alum, editor of *Relations: An Anthology of African and Diaspora Voices,* and author of *Powder Necklace*

"There are so many ways to grow your writing community. Online, social media is an easy way to connect with other writers. Offline, visit your local independent bookstore and chat up the booksellers. Learn about ongoing reading series in your area, attend an author event, or take a workshop. The library is a great resource, too!"

— MARISA SIEGEL, Girls Write Now Mentor and author of *Fixed Stars*

"In my opinion, friends and family aren't good readers— because they're familiar with your own biography, I like to say they "know all your tricks." It's also important to find readers who are also writers, who can give more constructive feedback. I can't think of a better place to start than within the Girls Write Now community, but there are also online platforms like Wattpad, Tumblr, AO3 (if you write fanfiction), Scrivener, etc."

— LIVIA NELSON, Girls Write Now mentor and writer

*How can I make sure the plot of my story is more than just a group of scenes thrown together?*

"You've heard most of the following before, but it bears repeating as it's the only bulletproof method to craft stories. At their core, all good stories are comprised of a **Beginning,** a **Middle,** and an **End.** Most importantly, each part of a story is led by Action and Conflict. Which can simply be defined as: What is your character trying to get and what is getting in the way of them getting that thing? Every. Single. Time."

— PRISCILA GARCIA-JACQUIER, Girls Write Now Teaching Artist
and television writer

"Write down a one-sentence synopsis of your story and put it in the header or footer of your draft. This way, as you write, you always have to ask yourself: How is this page reflecting and advancing the overarching story?"

— NANA BREW-HAMMOND, Girls Write Now Mentor Alum,
editor of *Relations: An Anthology of African and Diaspora Voices,*
and author of *Powder Necklace*

"This magic largely happens in revision. Look at the different plot threads in your story, consider color-coding them, even, and how they're spread throughout the piece. Is the story balanced? Are your primary themes touched upon in most scenes? How are you transitioning between scenes so your reader doesn't get lost?"

— MARISA SIEGEL, Girls Write Now Mentor and author of *Fixed Stars*

"The plot is similar to the roots of a plant. The roots are present and give the plant life, but you can't see them. It should be the same with your story. The plot is what the story is about but it need not be in the reader's face. Determine what your story is about, the highs and lows and how you are going to answer the story question: What do my characters want and how will they get it?"

— DONNA HILL, Girls Write Now Mentor Alum and author of
*After the Lights Go Down* and *Confessions in B-Flat*

### How can I successfully incorporate multiple themes or perspectives into my work?

"Characters are just like us, they have interests of all sorts, and sometimes they surprise you. So never be afraid to add a theme or perspective that feels particular or surprising, it might just make your character feel that much more uniquely themselves."

— MEREDITH WESTGATE, Girls Write Now Mentor and
author of *The Shimmering State*

*Visit www.girlswritenow.org/resources for more*

# PROFESSIONAL WRITING TIPS

### *How do I know when my piece is done?*

"I'm still trying to figure it out. Sometimes I feel like I don't want to talk about this no more so I'm done. In *Chlorine Sky*, I just wanted it to be a moment of revelation...because there's so much living to do, and I find that books that allow the reader to live a little bit longer in the text are the most healing."

— MAHOGANY L. BROWNE, Girls Write Now Teaching Artist, poet, and author of *Chlorine Sky*

"We kept on asking ourselves: is there anything we want to change about the poem? I learned that, yes, there is. There's a million things I want to change about it. And I forever will—because no piece of writing is ever complete. I think it's a beautiful thing to look back—maybe in a month or maybe even in a year—to see that there's so much more you want to say."

— ARIEL ZHANG, Girls Write Now Mentee and poet

"When you have gotten to the last page, when you have re-read the work and made your edits. When you have fulfilled your promise to the reader and your characters have achieved their goals."

— DONNA HILL, Girls Write Now Mentor Alum and author of *After the Lights Go Down* and *Confessions in B-Flat*

"I think a piece of writing is "done" when after rereading it for the nth time, I find myself switching back to a word or phrase, or exhuming something I've cut. To me, that signals the point when I am second guessing my "final" decisions. This said, I think, as writers, we have to get comfortable with the work never being "done," only finished so we can move on to the next work."

— NANA BREW-HAMMOND, Girls Write Now Mentor Alum, editor of *Relations: An Anthology of African and Diaspora Voices*, and author of *Powder Necklace*

### *How important is it to find people to read my writing and give me feedback? How can I find those people?*

"How do you choose your beta readers? Answer: Trust. You have to get someone who has time... they can commit to you in a way that you need. My readers, one of them is a journalist and a poet, the other is a teacher and a poet, the other one works in a hospital, but she loves to read."

— MAHOGANY L. BROWNE, Girls Write Now Teaching Artist, poet, and author of *Chlorine Sky*

"It's important. Not only your best friend or English teacher, unless they're a publisher or agent. Published writers sometimes read the work of new writers to give them feedback. Doesn't hurt to ask. There are groups of "readers" called Meta readers who also read work and give feedback. Google to find groups."

— JANIS KEARNEY, Girls Write Now Teaching Artist, author of *Only On Sundays: Mahalia Jackson's Long Journey*, President and Founder of Writing our World Publishing

# SELF-REFLECTION PROMPTS:

*How does reading pieces that relate to one another impact your experience of each of the pieces individually? How can your response to each "Tell Your Story" writing prompt allow you to continue the conversation that those pieces' authors are having?*

*Think of a scene from your life. What did that experience look like to another person in the scene? Explore their outlook by writing the scene from their perspective.*

# TRANSFORMATION

*You have to believe that you are already a writer. You don't need an MFA. You don't need to have a book out. You don't need a byline to be a writer. Own it today. Period. Because if you don't own it, you don't pursue it as if it is real. Because other people are going to doubt you. Let me tell you, I knew I was a writer back in like 2009, or at least by 2010. I was like, I'm a writer. Other people would tell me, "You know, you're not published, whatever. Oh, it's your hobby. Oh, you're looking for yourself."*

*I can see myself right here, like I have a mirror. What do you mean I'm looking for myself? I know where I am. You are a writer. And when you say, I am a writer, then you start taking steps to get closer to being published. I went into the MFA with three goals. I wanted to improve my craft, because as a writer, we can always improve our craft. I wanted community, because I knew community was important with other writers. And I needed—and this is key—mentorship.*

— KEISHA BUSH, Girls Write Now Teaching Artist and Author of *No Heaven for Good Boys*

# Pelo Malo

## BY SHYANNE FIGUEROA BENNETT, 2012

*CW: mentions of rape, sexual violence*

*I wrote this when I was first exploring my identity as an Afro-Latina girl. With the support of my mentor Nora Gross, it was also the first time I realized poetry can engage messy complexity.*

My hair, the tightly wound curls of the uneven afro I wake in. Met with comb and brush, water and cream, rhythmic tugging, strands pop as I mold my hair around a face twisted with frustration I do not understand. This face, laced with the same genes of my hair, my legs, my arms and the hands that on days too quiet contemptuously hold the flatiron to my hair. Smoke rises, hot metal searing each rebellious strand.

I look at myself and see traces of an Indian ancestor. With half-closed eyes, a faint glance of her, my great, great, great grandmother—the Indian from India, or maybe she is the one from further back, the Taino in Puerto Rico or Jamaica. I look in the mirror with eyes now wide in wonder. I touch my hair—soft and silky, thin and limp. So thick before—or was it? The remnants of him, my English ancestor—no, Scottish, my grandmother said. I wonder if he loved her. Did she love him, and did she love the Spaniard, too? Was it love or was it rape? I should ask her if the thinness of my hair was conceived in a beautiful or tragic moment. If tragic, what should I think when I straighten it? Should I see it as a relic of a broken past or the cryptic symbol of times forever forgotten. Long straight, thin hair or thick, curly short hair. All is me and not me. Perhaps, it is her.

When I admit my confusion in choosing aloud, I am told to relax my hair—the permanence in straightening. If I do, what will she say? Relaxer, taming the ancestor on the long boat ride, the one with the scars on her back, the one that watched it all and saw it all but could not change it all. Instead she held it in the locks of her hair and passed it on to her daughter who passed it on to her daughter and on and on, all the kinks and curls and waves, and now to me. What do I do with this? Carry it on. What does it mean to hold the flatiron up to my hair? What does it mean then, to uncurl my curls?

*Shyanne Figueroa Bennett is a Brooklyn poet and educator whose work has appeared in* Green Mountains Review, The Rumpus, The Acentos Review, *and other publications. She is a Columbia University MFA graduate and Fulbright awardee.*

# Frizzy Mane

## BY DENISE DOMENA, 2023

*This piece highlights the complex emotions towards one's hair type
and the journey to self-love.*

The bristles of the brush combed through the strands of Maya's thick hair. She gripped the edge of the chair tight and curled her dangling toes. "Ouch!" Maya groaned.

"Don't move!" her mother tapped her head with the wooden side of the brush to enforce the message. It didn't hurt, but the act provoked a tear to streak her cheek. "I'm almost done."

Maya watched in the mirror as her mother pulled back her hair into a tight ponytail. She could feel the skin near her temples stretch as her mother's grip tightened. Her mother gathered Maya's hazelnut hair into a bunch and made work of brushing out the ends of it. She could hear the static coursing through, transmitting a shivering sensation down Maya's spine straight to her toes. She watched as her once-curly hair from last night's wash began to grow and frizz.

Maya frowned at the fuzz ball that emerged from behind her face. Instead of a luxurious lion's mane that depicted a strong ruler to an entire kingdom, her mane resembled a dethroned king after a scuffle with its uneven patches.

Her mother now stood in front of her daughter, holding a large can of hairspray. "Close your eyes."

Happily, Maya thought. Staring at her hair any longer would only make Maya worry more. She hated to think what the kids at school would say when they caught a glimpse of the tumbleweed glued to the back of her head. If she entered the classroom backward, undoubtedly her classmates would assume they were in the wild west about to witness a duel.

With her eyes closed, she felt the mist consume her and began to wish she had covered her face entirely as the chemicals seeped into her nose.

Letting out a few coughs as her mother pushed down her baby hairs, Maya looked up at her mother. Her mother's hair was unlike hers. It was charcoal black, fine, and wavy. It cascaded loosely down her back effortlessly.

Maya envied it.

She wished her ancestors had gifted her with the same hair. Hair her mother was familiar with and knew how to tame instead of the beast that only seemed to grow and consume her face.

Placing her hands on her hips, Maya's mother let out a sigh. "All done." Maya looked from her mane to her mother's reflected gaze through the mirror and emulated her expression. One of defeat.

With her mother off to work, Maya scurried to the drawer of cleaning supplies and pulled out a dryer sheet, only one so as not to be missed. In front of the mirror, she smoothed the white sheet through her frizz and instantly became consumed by the fresh linen scent. Maya flattened her hair as best as she could with the dryer sheet and tried to convince herself her efforts were working. The internet told her the method would strip her hair of static and frizz the first time she searched online for a solution. Surely it must be true.

Not satisfied with the results, Maya began to braid her frizzy tail and fastened her work at the end. Turning her head from side to side, she felt proud of her long braid. It was only when she looked onward into the mirror that she did not like the person that stared back. With her hair slicked back and her puff now constrained into a twisted cord, she thought she looked like a boy.

Certainly not the look she had wanted, but the one that would have to do.

Perhaps she could ask her mother to get her hair straightened. Then she thought better of it, knowing the hair salon workers would charge extra given the length and thickness of her hair, complaining it was too much work. Besides, she didn't like her straight hair. Yes, it was manageable for the week in which it lasted, but Maya would always feel like an imposter. Only when her curls slowly began to surface did a wicked smirk inch its way onto her lips.

She didn't hate her curls. She thought they suited her. Only when her mother treated her hair as if it was her own hair type did it turn into something she disapproved of. Maybe it was time she started treating her hair differently if she wanted to see new results. A method that could ensure her curls stayed intact and kept the frizzy mane at bay.

Maybe the internet could provide a solution.

---

*Denise Domena (she/her) is a sophomore at Hunter College majoring in English. When she isn't reading or writing, you can find her crocheting while binge-watching shows.*

## Tell Your Story

### A Prompt from Denise Domena

Write about the type of person you see when you look into the mirror.

# My name is not my sky
## BY AMALIE KWASSMAN, 2008

*This piece is for all those who have ever felt silenced or
needed to fight to make their voice heard.*

My name is not my sky.
I am more than what surrounds me
I'll be more than that.
No matter how many times people try to take my voice away
I'll always fight them back.
Cause I'm still here
but I'm still beating, believing, breathing
with thunder thighs
and stolen eyes
while melting mornings are mourning
never silent sunrise.
But I'm still here
my name is not my sky.

And I will be more than what I see going on around me
and where I come from
even if love and being alive
never coincide
alabaster houses will forever collide
with struggling never explicitly stated but always implied
Never ask those who are living if they are breathing
Never ask the broken heart if it is bleeding
Swallowing my edible spring
while waiting for the real thing
of park swings,
spreading my wings
and exchanging wedding rings
still I sing
of the salsa dancer who left me her shoestrings to dance for her
trembling
lost

I will dance because they say, "you just leave the door ajar so that even if you
can't someone else is going to do gymnastics to her guitar"
but the witty ramblings of my hips
will never eclipse
all the sadness that exists
in never-parted lips of New York City basements
Narrow hallways
Pushing us farther and farther away
But
My name is not my sky. Anyway.

---

*Amalie Kwassman is a mentee alum working on her PhD in Rhetoric and
Professional Communication at Iowa State University.*

# From Above

## BY KATHRYN DESTIN, 2023

*This piece is about being courageous, reflective, and honest to overcome the obstacle of fear both from other people and within yourself.*

I hate being in the service industry. The high-pitched clinking of tiny hors d'oeuvres plates, lipstick-stained champagne flutes, and ornately designed dessert spoons ring in my ears whenever I drift to sleep. Every time I clock in, I get the unpleasant tight and crampy feeling wrought by anxiety over accidentally dropping the food and drinks valued higher than my one month's rent. And don't get me started on how awful rich people smell after 5 p.m. I wouldn't wish working in service on anyone.

I work at a rooftop bar and restaurant down by the pier. It's cool in theory, but not so much when you're like me and have a fear of heights. On every one of my elevator rides up to the 49th floor to Epsilon 47, I blast my music through my headphones and clench my jaw to distract myself from how light-headed I get and the feeling of my heart pumping through my chest. I got this job three years back when I was sixteen, and money was super tight at home. I thought I'd only be here a few months and figured I could stick it out, but when my parents told me I had to move out a few weeks after my seventeenth birthday, I realized I was in it for the long haul. I stayed at my aunt's house for a while to figure things out. By the time I turned eighteen, I deferred my enrollment into SUNY Binghamton for a year and got my own apartment I financed with more shifts and babysitting the kids of two teen moms from my high school. So, for a little while longer, I am fated to work in a New York City skyscraper despite my phobia of heights.

\* \* \* \* \* \* \* \*

I'm three months out from leaving for Binghamton and halfway through my 12 p.m.-to-10 p.m. Thursday shift contemplating sneaking a few drinks to give me some edge when I notice in the corner of my eye one of the Epsilon's regulars walk through the glass doors and grab a table. I go to greet him and offer him his usual neat scotch and tell him what the menu is for the night. As I get closer, I catch a glimpse of a woman standing next to him I don't recognize as part of his usual entourage of coworkers he comes here with after work. When I get to him and the mystery lady, his eyes light up with recognition of me.

"Hey there, you! I'll have the usual neat scotch and my lovely wife here will have a lemon drop."

"Oh, is this your wife?" I ask. He didn't peg me as a wife guy. "I'm so used to seeing you with your entourage."

He laughs. "Yeah, I know. I left the folks at the office to fend for themselves. I realized after all these years of talking about my nights at Epsilon, I've never actually brought my lady here."

"I've been hearing about this place since our SUNY Binghamton days twenty years ago when he stumbled on it during a weekend trip into the city," she chimes.

"Great, now she's doing calculations to figure out what an old fart I am," he says defeatedly.

"If it makes you feel better, I suck at math. I'm about to go to school for Anthropology, anyway. SUNY Binghamton, in fact." I share.

They laugh in unison at the coincidence.

"I'm sure you're going to have a blast at Binghamton," his wife assures me.

"I'm looking forward to it!" I respond.

"Hey, not too much fun, though!" my regular says in a somewhat fatherly tone.

She interjects, "Yes! Don't forget to slow down and smell the roses. Those four years fly by. Make sure to catch the sunrises, too! They're so much better out there than they are in the city. You just have to get up high enough to fully appreciate it."

"I have a thing about heights, but I'll make sure to check them out on the quad if I'm up early enough," I say.

"I used to have a thing about heights, too, until this guy here made me sneak up to the roof of the science building to watch the sunrise our sophomore year. He was really cute back then, so I played it cool when I saw how high we were. Plus, once that dark sky turned pink and orange, it was all worth it."

"Maybe I'll give it a go. I'll go get your drinks."

"Thank you," they both chime with a smile.

\* \* \* \* \* \* \*

It's the day before I head back home to the city to spend the winter break at my aunt's house. I made it out of finals alive and am chatting with my friends about our break plans over an early dinner. Just as we finish, one of them notices the sun is about to set and recommends we go sneak onto the roof of the old history building, which is rumored to have a faulty door that doesn't trip off the fire alarm.

"It's too cold for that," I tell her.

"Yeah, but we won't be long," she pushes back.

I cringe at the thought, but before I can say anymore, everyone agrees it would be a great way to celebrate the end of the semester. My friend grabs and squeezes my hand to comfort me.

I slowly follow along behind them and wonder to myself what kind of friends I've made over these last five months in my first semester at school. Once we reach the building, we climb a series of stairs and open the door to the roof, proving the no-alarm rumor true. We sit next to each other, huddled to keep warm in the coldness of mid-December in upstate New York.

Our usually talkative selves promptly fall quiet as the sun begins to set. We watch the sky become painted pink, blue, and purple. Suddenly, I think back to Epsilon 47 and how I never paid attention to the sunset because I was usually getting ready for or already working a night shift, too caught up to look out at the horizon. Watching the colors meld together, I am reminded of that one regular and his wife telling me about this very scene.

"What you thinking about, Sama?" my friend asks, wrapping her arm around my shoulder to pull me closer.

"Oh, nothing. I just didn't realize how much prettier the view would be from up here," I respond.

"Told you so."

---

*Kathryn Destin (she/her) is a Harlem native and creative storyteller who experiments with multiple mediums. She has a love for writing, cooking, arts & crafts, photography, and comedy.*

## Tell Your Story

### A Prompt from Kathryn Destin

Reflect on a time fear or a situation hindered your ability to do something you wanted to do. In your piece, describe the physical experience you underwent when you were afraid and discuss how you overcame it.

# All the Best Strangers Have Mommy Issues
## BY CLIO CONTOGENIS, 2009

*This is a piece about first impressions and their limitations, a reminder that there is always more to a person than what initially meets the eye.*

He lives on my floor, at the end of the second of the four hallways that branch out from the elevator like the legs of a spider. He strides down the hallway with his hands in his pockets, bouncing with each step as if his legs are too long to move his body efficiently. He is always dressed in the same black leather jacket, which exudes the musty, cigarette-tinged odor that comes from spending years in the same closet. He is the sort of tall, lean person who tends to mold himself into a door frame whenever there is one available. He is temporary, never really belonging wherever he is: a question mark, an eraser smudge.

I try not to look at him as we stand side by side, waiting for the elevator, for I know that if I do, I will be forced to tilt my head up, up, craning my neck to get a look at his serious, dark-featured face. And he would notice that—notice me staring.

I would not shrink from observing another stranger, but I cringe when I see him. His presence isn't particularly frightening; it just freezes the air. I know that the words I send across that expanse of ice-air to him will die of cold along the way. Whenever I see him, I'm suddenly extra-aware of my body, shrinking my hands into my pockets, crossing one leg over the other until I stand rather like a twisted-up stork. I want to vanish into myself and not have to face that somber mystery.

My dad almost met him once. Our doorman, Pete, tried to introduce them in the lobby of
our building.

"Hiya, Constantine," Pete said cheerfully. "Y'know, there's another Greek guy that lives on your floor. Want me to introduce you?"

"Oh, that's nice," my dad said as he brushed by, in an irritable mood, not bothering to notice the tall, slender figure waiting expectantly behind Pete. As he approached the elevator though, he did notice, and thought of going back to apologize for ignoring our fellow Greek, but the damage was already done. The man hasn't spoken to us since.

Perhaps it is this unending silence that gives me the impression of time slowing whenever I see him, of the temporary death of everything in sight.

When I was younger, I just assumed he was a big, mean man. He didn't show the delighted interest in me, or the automatic softening at the corners of the mouth that I inspired in all the adults I found worthwhile. I didn't think that there might have been a reason I never saw him smile.

Then, one day as I was coming home from school, I found my route to the elevator blocked. I looked up from the book I was reading.

On the way to the elevator in my lobby, there is a single stair, with a short iron railing. This stair has caused many problems, once almost leading to a lawsuit, and setting off a series of discussions and plans for the reconfiguration of the entrance to the building in hopes of making it more accessible. My strange neighbor stood just below the stair, holding the elbow of a very old woman with a walker, who was struggling to get down. They had clearly been there for a while. She was more of a ghost than a woman; she leaned all of her weight on him, unable to hold herself up, but there was so little of her that he bore it easily. Her bones creaked their way into position as she slowly shuffled her feet closer to the edge of the wide stair.

I once saw a movie in which there was a man whose bones were as fragile as glass. He lived alone in an apartment, swathed in numerous sweaters, his furniture and walls all padded to prevent some accidental collision from breaking him. As I watched my neighbor shift who I assumed to be his mother toward the edge of the stair, I wished that there was some sort of padding on the marble floor of the lobby, for if this woman were to fall, she would certainly shatter. I watched them until I realized I was watching, then hastily stepped back, trying to pretend I had only just entered the lobby. I looked down into my book again and skirted them to the elevator, escaping into its bland impersonality. I could not have been more embarrassed had they both been naked. I felt as though I had witnessed something painfully intimate, not meant for the eyes of anyone but the two of them. It wasn't just a man helping a woman down the stairs, it was a son living his mother's death. There was a raw, almost instinctual response to that image that I had no right to see.

I hadn't known his mother was dying. I tried to imagine what it must have been like for him, to come home every day to less and less of her, to find himself supporting the figure who had supported him throughout his growth. Was there a part of him that was seeping away with her, the air around him being sucked into the hole created by her approaching death?

Now I understood his unsmiling face. But this understanding didn't lessen his mystery. Instead, it made him seem all the more distant from me. The mere thought of someone I deeply loved dying was almost unimaginable. His endurance of her death elevated him to some higher level of experience that I could not reach.

Today, as the elevator doors open with a ding, our eyes meet. We both tighten our lips, stretching our mouths backwards into those flat, little smiles that pass between near strangers who accidentally acknowledge each other, as if we are apologizing for this temporary awkwardness.

We stand in opposite corners, and I can feel the air between us growing brittle with the silence. I focus my eyes firmly on the tips of my boots. I wonder if I can allow myself to look up to check what floor we are on, this ride is taking far too long, we must have gotten stuck. I let my gaze flick upwards. The elevator is moving down as it should, just passing the fifth floor. I look back down to my feet.

At last, the door swishes open and we are released. As we step out of the elevator, heading in opposite directions, I hear him speaking over my shoulder.

"Have a good day."

His voice is low, bottomless, like the sound of boulders scraping against each other.

"You too," I say automatically, then stop and turn in surprise. He is already leaving the lobby. I can't tell if he heard me.

---

*Clio Contogenis is now a professional actor (though she has kept her passion for writing alive). She is a graduate of Yale University and lives in Upper Manhattan with her two cats.*

# right where you left us

BY JAMILAH ARAF, 2023

*CW: school shootings / gun violence*

*"All the Best Strangers have Mommy Issues" stuck out to me because
of how it highlighted biases. A code blue at my school led me to
center the piece around the issue of gun violence.*

Taylor Swift's *right were you left me* echoed through her head as a crackly voice came over the speakers, interrupting a perfectly good free period. After all these years, the students could sing along with the announcement word for word, yet only the sub noticed the missing lyric. The students, on cue, rose from their chairs, but the show didn't truly begin until the lights went down. Tablets and computers shone like lighthouses, hoping to rescue the unsuspecting victims.

The sub did not push herself off the table, but instead floated from it until her feet delicately hit the tiled floor. Her bright red heels held their breath as she crossed the classroom ripping posters off the walls, and Emily watched this song play out in front of her. The lyrics had sounded the same as the countless other times she watched teachers perform it, yet somehow the melody, the delicate and quick pace, made it sound unfamiliar.

Emily finally recognized the song the teacher sang. She understood that the speakers did not forget a line, they simply sang another tune. As synchronized as a chorus, the whole class connected the pieces.

This was not a drill.

She froze. The realization should have sent her running, but instead she hid in plain sight.

She took the whole scene in, fixating on the details instead of being one. Lindsay, the popular girl who she assumed made fake friends for the numbers, had real tears streaming down her face wiping it clean. Lindsay buried her head in Lily's shoulder to hide her sobs from the reaper. Two tables over were Alexis and Jonathan. Emily never believed in teenage love (it was the work of crazy hormones, obviously), but the somber look shared between the two begged to differ. It was the same look Noah gave Allie, and it made denying their love impossible. On the very right, a coward just like her hid where the door would shield. She observed her crush (her hormones failed to obey her theory on teenage love) like he was a statue, all her feelings flying out the window. Months of long glances and eavesdropping convinced her that he was a level-headed, fearless man. How could this boy, crumpled on the ground like her doomed love letters, be the same one she dazed over? His tears flowed faster than blood from a gunshot wound. From across the room, his heavy breathing was suffocating her.

The main act, however, was the sub. Emily regretted not knowing the sub's name as she watched her walk back and forth to hide kids under desks and into lockers. She recognized the fear in the sub's eyes: hazel faded to blue as she recalled that sunny day when she and her sister were at the peak. Her sister turned to face her the moment the car started to plummet with those same eyes.

Both her sister and the sub knew the drop ahead. But everyone knew what was coming. It's why they gave their tears, their voice, and all of their potential to the tiles and tables that held them like the children they still were. The sub was an adult, following familiar choreography. She wasn't afraid of the dark like the kids were, but of what she knew it was hiding. And just like that, it felt as if this woman's clothes had unraveled, leaving her exposed to Emily. Emily could almost trace the sub's deep scars, ones she would never have the chance to develop herself. It felt wrong to watch the sub now, now that the dots had been connected. But she couldn't look away. She was watching a soldier return to her battlefield, prepared to see it sprinkled with bodies and blood once more. It was magical, and for that, it was frightening.

Luckily, she didn't have to decide whether or not to look away. The bullet did that just fine.

Isn't it so cool to see what a crisis can bring?
twenty-eight bodies

no need to look for a message

deeper than six feet

just move on
end the story
close the casket

STOP READING.

You're still here?
Fine, you want a bittersweet ending?
Here's a bittersweet ending.
Lily was buried with her favorite flowers,
tulips
(she never did care for lilies).

Alexis and Jonathan became known as
Mark and Lexie to the cool kids,
and Romeo and Juliet to everyone else.
They were what every high school couple strived to be.

Emily finally understood what her favorite song meant
and who that sub really was
even if she couldn't tell anyone.

The bittersweet ending is that this is a work of fiction
And that it will probably never happen to you.

---

*Jamilah Araf (she/her) is a high school sophomore with a love of poetry and swimming. She listens to her favorite artists every chance she gets and loves to geek out about her favorite characters.*

## Tell Your Story

### A Prompt from Jamilah Araf

Write a horror or thriller story
based on a love song.

*This conversation is between current Publishing 360 mentee Jamilah Araf and mentee alumni Clio Contogenis. Read Clio's piece "All the Best Strangers Have Mommy Issues" and read Jamilah's response "right where you left us" on page 151.*

**JAMILAH ARAF:** I love the piece, "All the Best Strangers Have Mommy Issues." It's amazing. I was interested because I don't usually write memoirs. I usually find them too vulnerable. I'm curious why you write memoirs and what you like about them?

**CLIO CONTOGENIS:** They are so vulnerable; that's so true. I think part of it came from the fact that I was maybe a little bit obsessed with my own issues when I was writing those things, but I think ultimately I find it really interesting to try and make sense of my life by writing about it. Things, events, emotions—all of those things have a strong impact on me. It helps me deal with it to write about it and figure out where there is an interesting story there. Or if there's an arc or something that I or other people could learn from it.

I guess I'm comfortable being vulnerable in that way. I think this has to do with being an actor as well. It's a lot of being eager to be emotionally vulnerable.

**JA:** When it comes to these personal stories, do you journal about them right away or do you like to sit down at a certain time to reflect?

**CC:** I guess it varies a little bit based on the story. It always tends to be in a moment when I really want to create something and there are just moments or emotions or events that stick with me and get kind of clogged in my system. A way to try and work through that or understand it for me has always been to try and write about it, and so I'll do a little bit of thinking or talking out loud. I talk to myself out loud a lot and do a little bit of journaling and then, usually, I'll try and write a piece about it. I'll write a very, very bad first draft, and then be like, okay, so now that I've exorcised those demons, what is it that I'm actually trying to say with this piece? Is there some nugget of truth or some arc that I can pick out to reframe it around? And then I will go back and try and make something actually readable as opposed to just my anxiety.

**JA:** Well, this piece was definitely readable. It was super enjoyable to read, I really loved it. What was the nugget of truth for this piece? I interpreted it as making assumptions, but I wonder if there's something you were struggling with that you wanted to convey.

**CC:** Yeah, it totally was. It came through! It's funny because I haven't thought about this piece in fifteen years but that's exactly the thing that I was stuck on. My whole childhood, encountering this man. I had been intimidated by him and sort of bothered by him because there was some darkness and some unfriendliness in him that I reacted to as a child and didn't try to understand at all and I just thought, *oh, it must mean that he is just like that. He's just sort of this dark unlikeable human being.* I made no effort to understand him, or why he might be like that, or to have any grasp of his interior life, and then I found out reasons why he might act that way. I just found out more information about him and it gave me this sense of his humanity. I was so struck by the difference between my first impressions of him and the reality of his entire human emotional life. I'd made assumptions, and I was wrong and it was uncharitable of me to make these judgments about this person whose existence I didn't know anything about. That was exactly what was sort of stuck in my craw, and that's what stuck with me about that story and why I had to write it.

**JA:** Do you still write?

**CC:** I do! I wrote a short fiction story, wildly enough, last year. You know how sometimes you get sort of possessed by some weird idea and then this story just comes out of you without you really seeming to have any influence on it? I did that, and I wrote this short story. A friend of mine and I are working on developing it into a short film as well right now.

**JA:** That's so cool. Has writing become more of a hobby or is it equal to the acting that you do professionally in your eyes?

**CC:** Equal to acting? It certainly is. How does one define a hobby? I guess, if we're talking about what I like, what my job is, when I get paid to do—I get paid to act and teach, but I think writing is still a hugely important part of my life. I still journal all the time because I feel like writing—and I say this all the time—writing helps me make sense of myself and the world. And I find reading a hugely important part of that too. I still write. I'm not as productive of a writer as I was fifteen years ago but I do still write. I'm also working on a novel with my dad, so yeah—I still write all the time.

**JA:** What drew you to acting? Was it something you always wanted to do, or did you kind of veer off a different path?

**CC:** I was doing school Shakespeare plays when I was nine. That was the first time I ever did anything acting-related. Which, I mean, think about the teacher who was like, *I'm going to teach a bunch of nine-year-old's how to do Shakespeare and put on a play.* This man's courage lives in my heart forever. I think my love of acting is in a lot of ways connected to my love of writing because it's all a love of how language can move through a person and affect change, and influence feelings, emotions, opinions. It's all about the power of stories. I had this experience when I was doing this version of *The Tempest* when I was nine, and I was realizing that the language was transforming me and I was feeling all these things that allowed me to do things that I didn't think I could do before, and then it was being very immediately transferred to this audience, who was feeling it as well and reacting to it. It's very similar to what writing does. I have a very visceral reaction to the power of storytelling. I find that acting is a way that I can really be a part of that. And I think it's sort of what makes us human.

Storytelling is a lot of where we contain the higher ways of thinking and feeling. Like the way that Romeo and Juliet met each other and fell in love, and then they were ripped apart and they died. The way that the story can reach and affect, emotionally, everybody on the whole planet—the way that storytelling gets us back to what is most essentially human about everyone. The way that we all have these same reactions, these same emotions that we feel based on a narrative, and we all are able to feel empathy for these characters and learn from their decisions. I think that that is part of what makes us human. It's part of how we learn, it's part of how we grow, it's part of how we get back to what is good about being human.

**JA:** It's interesting. I'm kind of in a writer's slump, so I kind of feel that when I read other people's work, I'm like, *oh my god, how did you write this?* And then I try to sit down and I'm like, *what the hell? This sounds like it's been written before.* Do you have any tips for writer's block?

**CC:** Yeah, if you find any great tips, pass them back onto me as well. If there were a magical solution to this problem, I think that all of us writers would be much less angsty people than we are. The way that I have tried to get out of writer's block is ironically to just write a lot. And then not judge it and not read it for a little while. Because if I write something, I will find that if I read it right after reading it, I will think it's absolute garbage and throw it away, but if I read it three weeks later, I'll be like, oh, actually, now that I'm distanced from it that sentence is pretty good. You'll find getting some distance from whatever you sort of vomit out allows you to see the merit in it, I think. I feel like creativity ignites more creativity. Once I start going, often I will write myself into good writing. I need to do twenty minutes of awful prose before I'm actually able to express myself well.

**JA:** Sometimes I edit while I'm writing. I'll be in the middle of it and I'll be reading a sentence eight times being like, *this is not a good sentence. What am I trying to say here?*

**CC:** My inner critic is the most active little witch ever. The best way out of writer's block is to try and ignore that creature and just try to get everything out. You know, just get it out now and you can critique it later.

**JA:** That's a smart tip! When you were writing this piece fifteen years ago, did you imagine yourself here now? Or did you imagine something completely different?

**CC:** Did I imagine that anybody would read that story fifteen years later and care about it at all? No. I was completely shocked. I thought that was somewhere off in the ether, never to be spoken of again, but I'm very moved. I mean, this is the power of storytelling! This is what I'm talking about. Something that I wrote and forgot about fifteen years ago and was like, that doesn't matter—for it to have an impact on you later? That's part of why art and storytelling is so important to existing as fully-fledged human beings in the world. It makes me emotional. It's very sweet. I did not imagine that I would be here.

There are aspects of my life that I dreamed of—that I would be able to continue existing as an adult as an artist. I didn't know that was necessarily going to be possible. But it was always my hope that I would be able to be a writer or an actor when I grew up. And I accomplished that. I was always with blinders on, not thinking about the other possibilities. But this is what I dreamed. And to some extent I've been able to accomplish that, so that's very exciting.

**JA:** That's inspiring actually, because everyone makes it seem like the arts are such a difficult sector to enter. That you can't live off it, or that it's a hobby or something you do in your free time. It's not an actual career. But you're doing it.

**CC:** I mean, it's certainly hard, but everything is hard. Life is hard. But life is also great and rewarding.

**JA:** I know you had your experience as a nine-year-old acting, which I imagine was adorable, by the way. But did you have any plays or movies that kind of pushed you to writing? Something where you were like, *damn, I want to do that?*

**CC:** I got very into Shakespeare as a child. That was one big one for me. I watched movies all the time; my parents had a little movie night on Fridays. So we would watch all of the classic films, the greatest films of all time. Watching as a child with my parents, I was like, *woah! How does this exist in my world? It's all so much bigger than me.* It was just very eye-opening.

I had a thing as a kid where I read a lot, but I was always very frustrated because all of the protagonists in all the stories that I read were boys. And I was like, where is a story about me? I would often change the name of the protagonist and pretend that it was a girl. And then I read the *His Dark Materials* series by Philip Pullman. I found that when I was seven or eight years old, and it was about a little girl. And she was the hero and went on all these really intense adventures and was very brave and complex and would struggle with all the things that I would struggle with, but knew how to overcome them. Reading that book and watching this gutsy little girl be thrown into a world that was much bigger than her and have the courage to take it on and to change the world was formative for me. That story really inspired me a lot. It made me believe that maybe I too could have some impact on existence.

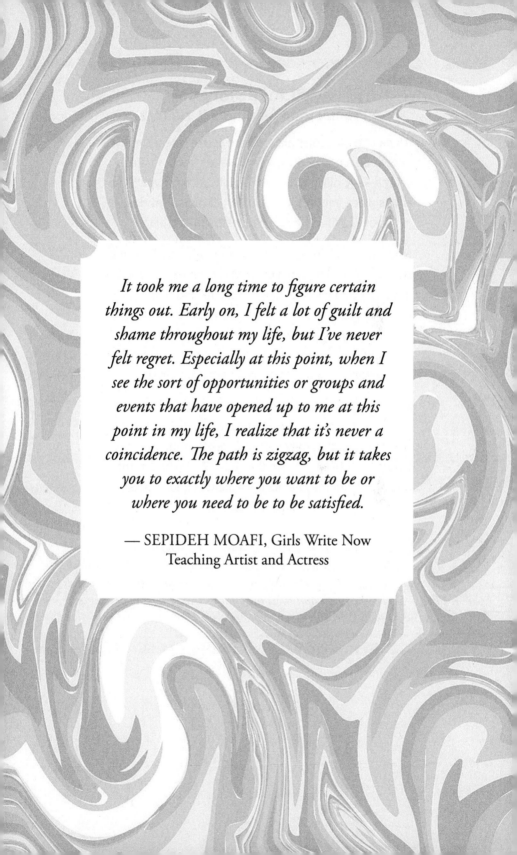

*It took me a long time to figure certain things out. Early on, I felt a lot of guilt and shame throughout my life, but I've never felt regret. Especially at this point, when I see the sort of opportunities or groups and events that have opened up to me at this point in my life, I realize that it's never a coincidence. The path is zigzag, but it takes you to exactly where you want to be or where you need to be to be satisfied.*

— SEPIDEH MOAFI, Girls Write Now
Teaching Artist and Actress

# Tell Your Story
## A Prompt from Alexandra V. Méndez

Think of a particular place where you've spent time. It could be a house, a room, a vacation spot, a train, a church—any place that holds significance for you! Why is this place important to you? What memories does it evoke? What is your relationship to this place?

Now imbue this place that you wrote about with some kind of magic. The way you do this is up to you. Maybe the place is magical because of the feeling that it gives off, or because of some seemingly impossible element or property. Or perhaps it is simply magical because of how you write about it—in the surprising similes, metaphors, adjectives, and verbs you choose.

Imagine a character who enters this magical place. The character is not you, though they may be similar to you. Do they feel that they belong here? Do they feel that they do not belong or are they unsure of whether they belong? Write the character's experience as they enter this magical space.

---

*Alexandra V. Méndez is a writer, teacher, and scholar who grew up bilingual in Decatur, Georgia, with family roots in Mexico and Mississippi. She graduated from Harvard University in History and Literature and has a PhD in Latin American and Iberian Cultures from Columbia University. What the Jaguar Told Her is her debut novel.*

# The Princess

## BY MARZIA SEEMAT, 2021

*A broken princess discovers a power that she held in herself from the beginning... But the question is—who is this princess?*

Once upon a time, there was a princess, with long dark hair, wide eyes, and a bright smile with a dimple on her left cheek. Unlike any other princess, she didn't have an Empire, nor a ton of soldiers, or a prince. All she had was an innocent heart—filled with pain. Her misty-eyed tears used to soak her pillow every night as she glared at the stars, quietly, from her small window.

All she wanted was for someone to listen to her; to understand her; to support her; to wipe her tears; to hug her tight; to not judge her like the rest of the world; simply for someone to love her. But all she had were inner demons, constantly fighting with her little heart, as it cried out silently inside.

This princess was unique. She was fake to the world, but real to herself; fake to the sun but real to the stars. She used to put fake smiles on around others, pretending to be the happiest soul alive. But only she knew about the deep scars each of her smiles left in her heart. She often found herself standing before the mirror, observing her crystal-clear reflection, where she always stood with a broken heart, a tired soul, and a shut mouth, along with her hollow eyes, which kept dropping blobs of tears. Maybe those tears were the only possible way for her heart to express its pain with her soul. Maybe her soul was looking for the real princess through her eyes, who got lost long ago trying to fit in among the worldly creatures. Or maybe her soul decided to be the one listening to her unspoken pain.

Every morning she wiped away her tears, trying to be wise, to be strong, to hold back her broken-heartedness. But no matter how much she tried, tears always managed to find their way back to her eyes. If pain taught her anything, it was to control her emotions in front of others. Because she knew no one cared. She knew about the self-centered characteristics of humans. She knew about the jealousy her smiles produced. She knew that others wanted her 'perfect' life, which she only pretended to live.

At one point, she got tired . . . tired of pretending . . . tired of forcing . . . tired of presenting herself as a different person before her loved ones. It seemed like she became a complete stranger to the people she shared her life with. She wanted to change that. She wanted to reveal herself...her pains, her struggles, her insecurities—her true-life, the Real Princess. But what could she do? None of them asked; they all got fooled by her forced smiles...

What else could she do other than fake those smiles? Ignoring her confusing memories was difficult. Sometimes they left her with a feeling of beautiful warmth. But mostly, they left her with ache and nostalgia.

Those dark memories used to be her weaknesses until she learned to let them fuel her. She taught herself to wipe away her own tears because no one else would. Now she started to look into the mirror without a swollen face but with sparkling eyes; now she admired the stars at night. After all, the stars were the only ones who had seen her every night, dragging herself to sleep. They were the only ones who saw her without her fake mask. They were the only ones who knew about her deep-dark pains, which she carried all day. They were the only ones with whom she could let her heart speak, in its own language. After a long time, those shining luminaries up in the sky got to see this princess sleep without a puffy face or a drenched pillow.

It is often said, when the heart wrings with pain, hatred is the only thing that offers a hand. The same thing happened for her. Those pains crossed the limit of her tolerance. So hatred took the place instead. But this time, she didn't hate herself. She didn't blame herself like before. She didn't force herself to wear a fake mask for others. She didn't let herself run into the life-maze again. This new princess *finally* learned to liberate herself. She refused to let anyone or anything control her besides herself; not even a memory. She repelled everything that would cost her even one droplet of tears. She started to use her inner storms, which she held in herself for so long, as her weapon. A weapon that would let her sleep peacefully again. A weapon that would bring her smile back. A weapon that would wipe away all her pain. A weapon that would bring back her innocent soul, but this time with a new version. A completely distinct version of herself who will not get betrayed again, will not get manipulated again, will not get lied to again. Someone who will not get bullied, neglected or threatened again; someone who will not feel abandoned, played, or hurt again. Someone who will not waste her precious tears again. Someone who will not allow the world to shatter her again.

*Marzia Seemat is a High School Junior in Brooklyn, who is passionate about love, elegies, social justice, and the world surrounding her.*

# Unwilling Royal
## BY SHADIYA BECKETT, 2023

*Someday throughout their lives, everybody develops inverted glasses
to look within themselves to find a purpose. This princess, now
coming of age, who has just developed her glasses,
is learning to live outside her ascribed status.*

There is always a princess with long dark hair, wide eyes, and a bright smile who, despite her beauty, does not feel the glow within her, but this princess is very different.

She floats away to an alternative universe, where imperfections mean beauty, where anger means passion, and where heartbreak means love. Her long dark hair, wide eyes, and bright smile save her every day when she looks in the mirror and sees all the flaws that she loves.

She has never felt the royalty so unwillingly bestowed upon her by birth, yet she feels the power to wear a crown of thorns as her tiara and not constantly whine about the pain she experiences. Yes, she yearns for support, but she knows she can stand on her own. Yes, she yearns for love but feels just enough on her own to make it through the day.

Her instability carries her to a place of unfounded tranquility because she knows nobody here is perfect, and that's exactly what she dreads becoming.

Every day, as she wipes her tears, she rubs in the knowledge gained from her experiences. She has no intention of being desired, nor does she desire anyone. The one thing she does want is a listening ear. She feels alone and ignored, but as long as she can hear her own thoughts, she is content with herself.

She wasn't always broken. She was once the perfect princess who had the perfect fairytale life. She believed in tooth fairies and all things magical. She had no worries nor cares. But as she grew into the world, she grew into the knowledge that life is nothing but a series of forced decisions and unfair opportunities. But after all the sorrows she has experienced, she decides to step out into the light for the first time in a long time.

*I knew I wasn't destined to be a princess. I always hated the idea of being locked away in a castle that had no personality, only perfection. I was desperately trying to start afresh, and as I looked up for an extra bit of strength, I found the sunrise doing the same. I was heavily mesmerized by how the colors danced with themselves, how the red faded into the yellow to make an impossible shade of pink, and how the blue stepped out of the spotlight just enough to blend in with the others. I lost myself in the beauty of nature and found myself on a ghostlike stroll toward the park.*

*All eyes were on me, but somehow I still felt invisible. I was misplaced, and everybody knew that. But nobody knew where I wanted to be or where I truly belonged. I didn't know either. All I knew was, at that moment, I felt like a regular person. The ground beneath my feet wasn't made of pure gold, and for once in my miserable life, I felt the freedom to breathe. It was then that I knew I didn't have to force myself into conformity. I didn't have to worry about faking a smile because nobody here was smiling. I could rip my broken heart out of my chest and display it to the broken world because everybody here knew what that felt like. Most of all, I didn't have to wear a crown of thorns because nobody here wore crowns. Everybody here was misplaced. Everybody belonged to nothing, and nothing belonged to everybody. Hurt and shame were expected, not repulsive or avoided.*

*At any moment before this, I would have broken down at this feeling. What is the point of living if I expect to be hurt? What is the point of hope if I must always brace for disappointment? Why must I hold back my tears just to let them out when I've reached my threshold? Why must I be happy knowing that it will not last forever?*

*I was a princess without a throne; a princess without the crown; a princess without a prince.*

*I was a princess in my own world. I never had the army of an empire, but I always had the strength of a thousand soldiers. I was a princess whose thoughts and emotions collaborated to confuse me. I had one thousand thoughts rushing through my head, battling for the forefront of my mind. I didn't know whether to celebrate my newfound liberty or grieve the truth, but for some reason, it all felt empowering. I felt normal.*

*And for the first time, I caught a reflection of the real me in the pond by the park. I could finally see the pain in my eyes. I was no longer numb, but I could actually embrace the pain. It was no longer fuel for my anger or resentment but reason enough to feel real. Real to myself, real to the world, real to the sun, and real to the stars.*

---

*Shadiya Beckett is currently a high school junior who typically expresses their profound affinity for writing through poems and songs, although they're not afraid to venture into unfamiliar genres. They also love dancing and interior designing.*

## Tell Your Story

### A Prompt from Shadiya Beckett

Write about an experience that changed the way you viewed yourself and your role in the world around you.

# Cycles, Words, Spirit, and Flow
## BY NAOMI HABTU, 2019

*I get really anxious about writing, so I decided to write about being anxious.*

**Cycles**
Every morning the sun announces a new day
Every night the sky falls over you like a blanket
Every day you wake up and soak in the air around you
As it goes through your lungs and into your bloodstream
Every second your cells regenerate allowing you to evolve

The tides roll in just enough to kiss your toes with a cold touch

The gears of this world are always turning
Never stopping
Never waiting for you to catch up

Grab sand from the hourglass
Stop the gears from turning
It slowly slips between your fingers
Grain by grain

The tides roll in just enough to kiss your toes with a
cold touch

Don't try to stop the sand from spilling
For the grains will always drop one by one

Every morning the sun announces a new day
Every night the dark sky falls over you like a
blanket
Every day you wake up and soak in the air around you
As it goes through your lungs and into your bloodstream
Every second your cells regenerate allowing you to evolve

Soak in the air around you
Don't grab the sand, don't grab the

Sand
Just let it fall
You can't stop the clock from ticking
The hands will keep moving
But you can continue to move just as it does

## Words

I used to effortlessly spit out words onto paper
Letting stories unfold
The song came naturally
Like the hums of a hummingbird spreading its wings
But now I have to dig
Dig deep into the earthly ground
With dirt, rocks, and worms
Preventing me from reaching my words
And when I am so close
They fall deeper into the ground
Right when I was about to reach out
And grasp them

## Spirit

I try to hold you like a thin piece of glass
Hanging on to your smile, your love, your essence,
Afraid they will blow away in the wind
But sometimes my palms get sweaty
So, I try to catch you before you crash
Your image is blurry, my mind stays numb, mixing memories I try so hard
not to forget
But it's hard to see you when you're not there
It's hard to hold on to something when it's not physical

## Flow

When I think of you,
I feel sunlight shining through my heart.
Through my arteries, through my veins
The warmth and golden light reaching every part of my body. Thinking of
you makes me smile,
I look up at the sky and smile,

I look up at the clouds, picturing you smiling down at me, and
     I smile.
But then my smile fades away when I remember that you are
     up there
And I am down here.
It makes me happy to know that you are up there,
But sad to know that we are not together.
God lifted you up, and now you are in eternal serenity
And I am here missing you,
Missing you forever until I join you,
I hope I will join you.
Until then that sadness spins into teardrops that fall from
     my eyes,

And roll down my cheeks and go past my mouth so I can taste
     the salt.
The bitter, sour, salty, taste of my tears resembles my feelings
     inside,
All mixed up making my stomach feel uneasy.
Sometimes I cry so much I can barely breathe.
I struggle to inhale oxygen and exhale it.
I struggle to let it in and let it out.
I feel like I am drowning as I am gasping for air.
I struggle to feel the pain, let it in, and let it out.
In and out
In and out, as I struggle to breathe.
My chest moving up and down
Trying to catch the air chasing for it.
Let it out.
But always after the storm winds down,
I breathe.
I can breathe.
I can let it in
And let it out.
My mind feels clear as if the gray clouds that poured out heavy
     tears have cleared up.
Leaving an arch of colors left to marvel at.
After I let it out, I can let it all in.

Let all the beauty of my surroundings in.
My smile slowly returns when I remember that you are up there,
But you were once down here,
And I am eternally grateful to know that I knew you,
And that you were mine.

---

*Naomi Habtu is a Girls Write Now mentee alumni and writer based in New York City.*

# Refractions

## BY CAMILA BONILLA, 2023

*A contemplative piece about the vulnerability
in writing about what you know.*

Every story is my own. Despite my desire to stray as far away as possible from my own world and what I know, I find that elaborate and well-researched characters somehow still resemble me.

If I look into a shattered mirror, I will still see myself, although fragmented and in pieces. My writing is the same. It is not a chronological story but rather a collection of moments, so somebody else can come and put the shards together. I don't expect whoever happens to stumble upon my mess to try to fix it. But I appreciate anyone who sees all of the silvery slices as something that was once whole.

A banded rainbow curls onto the white tablecloth through the glass of water. The shape morphs as different people and animals walk past. Even the trees rustling through branches shift the light. Everything in its vicinity changes the colors and the shape despite only water sitting in the glass.

The water is pure, and I try to keep it pure. It stays just water, but the way I see light around it changes. That is something I could never control. Light is how humans perceive everything visually. Is the water no longer water if light changes it so much that I can no longer recognize it as a liquid? Is that story still mine, even after distorting its original form so much that I can only hear my cries through dissonance?

When I write, when I really get into it and I feel like a spider spinning its own web, as if by instinct, a part of my brain turns off. Which is entirely hilarious because one would think that the entire attention span of your mind must be dedicated to the screen. In fact, I think that thinking inhibits true writing. Thinking too deep about the words I write creates sentences that are rigid and limited. Ones that hide the reality or truth of the matter. I don't know if my thinking makes this happen because I'm hesitant to uncover the truth, and put it into actual writing or because I don't know that it exists yet.

Color,
A fury in my mind,
Can I make it something that is real,
Do I have the strength to make it,
So real

Sometimes when I read something that is so raw and so real, I imagine what it will be like when I do that. When I become old enough to confront everything—age really matters in that process. Sometimes it feels like I am too young to know anything. I admire authors that use explicit and bold language and put it forth, when they put their whole name behind that piece of work, and stand by it, stand by all of the realness.

Is it them? I want to ask the authors. That part, the one that would have made me uncomfortable to write but somehow proud to make it something tactile, would have to come from within me and my own experiences. Most of my uncomfortable writing makes me uncomfortable because it is about me, and is me. I wonder what other people who know me will think about me when they read my writing, and get uncomfortable because they know for me to write that sentence, it had to exist somewhere in my mind for me. Even if entirely fictional, I had to imagine uncomfortable scenarios and relate myself to it. I try to put myself in just the right proximity to be able to do it and write it well.

I want to surround myself with those who are equally disturbed, but not enough to regard my experiences as uncanny. To feel that same discomfort and reel in that feeling with me, and somehow identify with it. This is the audience I desire in the future, when I publish my novels and short stories and poems. Maybe you are one of these people.

I fill up a glass with cold, cold water. I hear the pouring sound, and no steam follows after. It is just cold and acts like a prism with the light coming into my kitchen. This only happens on certain occasions. I rarely get to see a true sunrise, and have it filter through my windows like that. The outside is barred by two large stone walls creating a narrow pathway. Light passed through so many places for it to get to my cup. It traveled eight minutes through space, pierced the atmosphere, tunneled through the alley outside of my building and then shone, a temporary and fleeting glow, into my glass.

I saw rainbows in my cup, and it moved around and around based on its environment. Then it was just a glass of water, when the sun finally escaped the alley.

---

*Camila Bonilla is a high school senior in New York City. She loves to read and express her creativity by making films.*

## Tell Your Story

### A Prompt from Camila Bonilla

What are you most scared to write about?
Why are you scared to write it?

# Tell Your Story
## A Prompt from Christina Olivares

Take anything that you've written and be intentional about the placement on the page. How does moving words around on the page change the meaning? Where will you choose to place your words?

---

*Christina Olivares is the author of* Ungovernable *(YesYes Books, 2021),* No Map of the Earth Includes Stars, *winner of the 2014 Marsh Hawk Press Book Prize, and the chaplet Interrupt (Belladonna\* Collaborative, 2015). Olivares is the recipient of a BRIO Nonfiction Grant, a Lower Manhattan Cultural Council Residency and two Jerome Foundation Travel and Study Grants. In 2019, Olivares was an inaugural AAWW Witness Fellow. Her work has been published widely, including in* The Rumpus, Aster(ix), *and by The Academy of American Poets. Olivares has taught as a visiting professor at the Rutgers-Newark MFA poetry program. She earned her undergraduate degree at Amherst College in interdisciplinary studies in education, an MFA in poetry at CUNY Brooklyn College and is pursuing a PhD in English Education at Columbia University. She has worked widely throughout New York City as a youth worker, college counselor, teacher, and administrator. She is a poverty and prison abolitionist and queer, mixed American-Cuban from the Bronx in NYC.*

# Lonely, Womanly

## BY JOLIAMOUR DUBOSE-MORRIS, 2018

*This piece journals the awkwardness and discomfort of the transformation of the teenage girl to young woman. It's about confidence, it's about self-love, it's about bus rides, it's about right now, and it's about forever.*

*THE WORLD IS SMALL,* microscopic, dense, and it's intense. The cities aren't as big as one perceives them to be. Yes, there are streets and alleyways, and the buildings cave inward like pop-up cards on Valentine's Day. Except I've never received a card from anyone other than my mother.

*THE PEOPLE ARE SO LARGE,* I wish I could peel my skin off and try someone else on for a change.
      Yet that is not possible,
I guess I'll have to grasp onto myself, and what's left of it, and grow into a woman to be, even if the small child beneath her isn't okay with where she is, and where she's supposed to be.

      My eyes are burning, as if they are washcloths getting ringed out so tight. I still right my wrongs.
Womanhood vastly approaches like the alarm clock
we knock over when it dawns six and sleep has to be postponed because right now, morning calls.

      The duties of humanity are to talk and socialize but I disguise myself in various hairstyles and teary eyes. I'm not acquainted with Womanhood but she sits at the table of adulthood and cocks her brow with a poise that I've always dreamed of having. Womanhood and I will never be friends because she holds a better resumé and is ready to perform her flirtatious repertoires.

      I've said it before, I am afraid to grow up,
      yet it dawns on me that Womanhood is the first to show up, her hugs warm and motherly, but I don't need another mother, I just want more friends. I wander through the world like a solemn ghost with wild hair, and everyone sits next to everyone else while I'm that one that doesn't know what or who I belong to, unless I'm supposed to remain by myself.

No matter where I am,
silence saunters sonorously around me
and it weighs, and    w

           e

        i

      g

    h

  s.

The cities are so small, but the density comes from the intensity of the amount of people existing around each other. Then there's me. Somewhere in between being a kid and a woman, kind of lost, and kind of found, but unsure of what foot to step with next. Womanhood sits on the bus, and she sits beside me, and whatever comes after that, is unwritten history, perhaps.

---

*JoliAmour DuBose-Morris is a twenty-one year old writer, film nerd, and tortellini lover from Queens. She currently resides in San Francisco. She has worked with StyleCaster,* Document Journal, InStyle, *and more.*

# Forever, Girl

## BY KAYA FRASER, 2023

*The answers to girlhood's biggest quandaries aren't as elusive as
they seem to be—or perhaps they are. Only time tells.*

It had been seeping out,
slipping through browned cracks in mirrored walls.
Myself, she's sticky with falsehoods.
Half-truths and honest lies.
Delusion fragrant and dreams tangible.
I turn outward, then inward, upside down and back again,
searching, sifting through the cast out amidst the once lost.
I find Her.

*You wear your hair in a bob now. You grow into your forehead, though not as
much as you'd like. You look love in its faces. You cross murky waters you believed
you'd drown in. Sometimes you run for the bus. Sometimes you let it pass you.*

Was it ever really mine if I never knew I owned it?
Til I loaned it, sent myself out,
didn't know I was the lender, the spender.
She is— I am adrift.
Grasping at paper straws,
submerged in seas of what could be instead of what is.

*You never stop fearing that others will hurt you. You hurt too. You accept apologies
you never received. And you will find that you are your favorite friend. Sometimes
you run for the bus. Sometimes you let it pass you. The stop never moves.*

Truth is seeing blue for blue and yeses for maybes.
Swallowing the purple pill of uncertainty,
and planting your feet in loose soil, settling in quicksand.
The self does not bend to time's clock,

for She ticks to no tune and always is,
writes the invisible verses to the songs that we are.

*Sometimes you run for the bus. Sometimes you let it pass you. The stop never moves, yet you do.*

*Brooklyn-born, Kaya Fraser (she/her) is a Howard University alumna—a 2023 graduate with a degree in English. Her life's mission is to know joy.*

## Tell Your Story

### A Prompt from Kaya Fraser

Is growing older what you imagined it'd be? Reflect on younger you's hopes for the future. Write a piece that answers childhood's biggest questions.

## Tell Your Story
### A Prompt from Darien Hsu Gee

Choose someone in your lineage, by blood or by choice
or by inspiration. What are your connections to this
person? Search for emotional truth, a small revealing
of yourself or somebody in your life, real or imagined,
or an intense moment that may have changed you or
triggered a significant or pivotal moment.

What would be the first line of a poem or essay about
your family history or your artistic lineage? Once you
have your first line, finish your poem, or aim to write
your essay in 300 words or less. Title the piece when
you are done. As with all prompts, follow where it leads
and don't worry if you stray or go down a rabbit hole.
Explore whatever shows up on the page.

Now, if you wrote a poem in the last exercise, take a few
minutes to revise it into an essay in 300 words or less. If
you wrote a micro essay, take a few minutes to revise it
into a poem. Which version do you like better?

The final step is to revise the piece back into its original
form. Don't look back at the first exercise you wrote, but
take the second exercise and decide what you'd need to
do to put it back in the same original form you wrote,
poetry or essay/prose poetry. You can then compare
what you originally wrote to the revised version and see
what changed, what remained.

*Darien Hsu Gee is the author of five novels published by Penguin Random House that have been translated into eleven languages. She won the 2019 Poetry Society of America's Chapbook Fellowship award for* Other Small Histories *and the 2015 Hawai'i Book Publishers' Ka Palapala Po'okela Award of Excellence for* Writing the Hawai'i Memoir. *She is the recipient of a Sustainable Arts Foundation grant and a Vermont Studio Center fellowship. Gee holds a B.A. from Rice University and an MFA from the Rainier Writing Workshop at Pacific Lutheran University. Her most recent book,* Allegiance, *is a collection of micro essays about family, motherhood, and growing up Chinese American. She lives with her family on the Big Island of Hawai'i.*

# Life in Odd Numbers

## BY MARQUISELE MERCEDES, 2015

*And in your bones, you know they will stay with you always.*

### Three

The hours on a bus from Albany to the City. It is twenty-one dollars for a ticket, not including the train ride uptown into spray-painted subway signs and late-night service delays. Your sister rolls her black duffle bag through the melted snow on the cracked pavement, ignoring the guys who stand at the corner of Gun Hill Road and Burke Avenue. There is one there who proclaims his love on a regular basis—both directly and indirectly. Yet, she has no time. Franderis moves too fast for his feet and his mind, leaving him to choke on her icy dust. So does she. The cold air constricts her asthmatic airways and makes her wheeze. When she arrives at one in the morning—brown cheeks stained with pink, black hair plastered to her sweaty forehead—she kicks the front door with her boots.

### Five

The number of twenty dollar bills your mom spares to gift you on your birthday. They are in separate envelopes; the silver-and-black-striped enclosures are embedded with generic phrases like "it's your special day" with too many exclamation points. Her fine, brown fingers cradle the sides of your head and your bashful "thank you" is lost to the sound of her smacking kisses on your frizzy hair. The custom-made ice cream cake is at the center of the table in front of you, butchered by a hot knife, oozing dulce de leche. It lies beside a present you have yet to open. You wonder in dread how much it cost, but then remember you were born during income tax season. Your stomach stops its churning.

### Seven

The charms on your bracelet that tinkle like small wind chimes when you move too enthusiastically. You remember how you got each and every single one. The retro sunglasses for the white sand beach of Punta Cana. The crescent moon clip to match the ink behind your ear. The dangling butterfly and heart, both imbued with feelings of "forever." Each one inspires deep, vigorous love—the kind that rushes through you like rapids and threatens to swallow you up when you're lonely. They constantly remind you that you are not—lonely, that is—but you find yourself pushing into the corner of your room, making friends with the loose threads on your stuffed cow. They've come to grips with the fact that it's just who you are.

### Nine

The grade you slipped on a slope peppered with spikes. You are left with shredded insides and weak legs and a broken mind and it is hard to get back the breath that is knocked out of you. You start to let your mom stroke your hair when the pain is too much and reluctantly admit that you like it when you are left alone and she is at work. At the bottom of the slope is a dark pit and you are in it for three years. At first, you are too broken to try to climb out. You get comfortable on the mold-covered ground, ignore your sour stench, and eat what can stay down. But when you finally hear them calling your name, you start to claw at the walls. Your brain blocks the climb out, but you suck in the fresh air greedily, hear them cheer despite the fact that everything is different and you are not perfect. And when your feet continue to dangle over the edge of the pit, they do their best to help you not fall in again.

### Eleven

The hour you were born. Your mom says you and your sister were clean and shiny. Your father is too late to cut your umbilical cord, but that is okay because he doesn't fit in with the rest of the story anyway. Your sister wonders why you are so much lighter than she is, but she still loves you. You can see it in an old, unfocused picture probably taken by Mom. Franderis holds you like she's supposed to and the gap between her two front teeth is brilliant. And in your bones, you know they will stay with you always.

*Marquisele Mercedes is a Girls Write Now mentee alumni from New York City. She attended the Dewitt Clinton High School in the Bronx, and Hunter College in New York City.*

# Recipe for Aging: Just Add Teen

## BY SIA KORTEQUEE, 2023

*Age is such a crucial number in life.*

### Thirteen

Seems to be an unlucky number. Many hotels and establishments don't have the thirteenth floor. No one wants to be thirteen, except for me... When you turn thirteen you are officially a *"teenager." I'm officially thirteen,* you say to your mom. Yet you don't feel any different. The bus leaves at 7:13 A.M. carrying the thirteen cupcakes you baked for each of your friends. Each cupcake has a number on it. I hoped to pass them out in chronological order of when I met each friend. At 8:13 I start to walk down the steps of the bus, one two *three* ... I am on the floor and my cupcakes go from *13 to 3*. Laughter from my peers floods my ears as I pick myself up and run into the school, my eyes burning with tears. Thirteen is truly an unlucky number.

### Fifteen

The age you were when you realize how independent you can truly be. It's September of my sophomore year. All of my teachers expected us to be completely independent. When you are struggling it is supposedly known that a parent cannot speak for you. When help is needed, you seek it out by yourself, no matter how scared you are. My mother and I never got the memo. When honors classes became a struggle, the teachers ignored my mom's emails and texts. Instead, taking it out on me. "I don't deal with parents." "If you need help, talk to me," they said. I was frozen in fear. Fear of failure. I felt *five*, not *fifteen*. When you are just *fifteen* asking for help is embarrassing. I was just fifteen.

---

*Sia Kortequee (she/her) is a writer from New York City. She enjoys track and field and listening to music.*

## Tell Your Story

**A Prompt from Sia Kortequee**

How have you noticed people responding to you or
interacting with you differently based on your age? Can
you remember when people seemed to start treating you
differently once you reached a certain age? At a certain age
did you anticipate or yearn to be treated a specific way?

# Riding Unicorns

## BY SHIRA ENGEL, 2009

*If you want to come find me, I'll be with the unicorns.*

I asked Mommy if, when I die, or if, when you die, I would live with her or you in heaven. She told me there is no such thing as heaven so I asked her if I would live in hell. She told me there is no such thing as hell. I asked her where I would live when I die. Only then Mommy looked up from her newspaper. She rubbed her forehead, then stared at our refrigerator. I can't read minds, but I could tell she was counting to ten in her head like she tells me to do when I might say something people won't like.

"When you die, you don't live anywhere."

"But Tommy told me his grandparents moved to heaven last week."

"Lily, when you die, you just don't live."

Mommy stared at me and then at her newspaper again. She told me she had a headache, which is what grown-ups say when they don't want to answer any questions. You never had headaches.

You answered all my questions, but maybe grown-ups can only answer a certain number of questions and then they have to leave. Maybe you left because you used up all your answers and had to go find more. I'll bet Mommy had a headache because she needs to stay and take care of me so she can't use up all her answers yet.

Anyways, I didn't understand how someone could just not live. But then I thought about when I turned seven and got too big to play in the sandbox in the park. One day the kids playing in the sandbox looked so small. Mommy took my hand and whispered that I was just too big for it. So that must be what death is like. You can't play in the sandbox when you're seven and you just don't live when you die.

I looked at Mommy again and thought that one more answer should be okay so I asked her if, instead of going to heaven, I could just go with the unicorns when I die. She told me I could just ride the unicorns as she filled a word in on her crossword puzzle. I knew she wasn't taking me seriously because she said the *i* in *ride* for a really long time, like a cat's cradle string she stretched through her fingers without even thinking. Maybe, since she wasn't paying attention to me, that answer won't count.

The thing is, if I won't see you in heaven I don't know when I'll ever see you. I already had a whole plan in mind. Heaven would be like the circus, only without the clowns. Maybe if you knew that you wouldn't have left because you would have known that we would never see each other again.

Do you know why heaven would be the circus? The last time I saw you, it was two years ago and I was so young. You took me to the circus. Remember? Don't worry; I know you do. We took the train all the way into London! We went into a gigantic blue and white tent that looked like a football stadium in outer space from inside. There were a hundred clowns. I wasn't afraid of them.

There were elephants and tigers and old men in orange suits holding hula hoops. There were probably more animals but our seats were so high, I felt like I could have touched a star.

When the circus started, you left to go to the bathroom. You wouldn't know this, but the circus was pretty boring at first. It was cool to see the first tiger jump into the hula hoop, but it got old after a while. I just sat there, stuck in my seat that was so squishy that if I looked straight out, the first thing I saw were my jellies sandals.

And then, you came back from the bathroom holding a white stick with bright green cotton candy! I remember you sat down and dropped the stick in my lap accidentally. I didn't mind, though. I picked it up and ate it. Sometimes I think I can still see the green mark on my overalls, but it's not really there. You see, that night, after you left, I saw Mommy washing them in the sink and she said tears fight stains best.

I sat there eating the cotton candy when you whispered something in my ear.

"Look at the unicorns," you said.

A nice lady in front of us passed me her binoculars, but I just saw horses on the stage.

"Unicorns are horses with wings and horns on their heads," you whispered.

I think that's what I remember best about that day. The unicorns. That night I dreamed I rode one of them. I petted its mane and lifted my arms wide and flew through the clouds. It looked so nice I wanted to just ride them all the time, but I would return to the circus sometimes, if it meant eating cotton candy with you.

I guess I won't see you in heaven after all. If you want to come find me, I'll be with the unicorns. Well, they're just horses with painted sticks drilled into their skulls. So just look for me in the circus. I'll be the one riding the horses, holding on to the painted stick so I won't fall before you see me.

---

*Shira Engel was a mentee with Girls Write Now from 2006 to 2010. She holds a BA from Wesleyan University and an MA from Columbia University. She is now a middle school Humanities teacher, Wilson-certified dyslexia practitioner, and curriculum creator.*

# Thoughts on Death
## BY IFEOMA OKWUKA, 2022

*Sometimes, the most incomprehensible things in life make
for the most powerful discussions.*

Dear Shira,

Death is unfathomable. And like all things unfathomable, my understanding
of it can only be helped by exploring its inverse: life. The funny thing is that
life is unfathomable too. And if I cannot answer what it means to be alive,
what hope is there in deciphering death? In Riding Unicorns there exists
this overarching theme of engaging with the incomprehensible. Lily does not
understand how it is that "someone could just not live." I too cannot understand how someone can simply cease to exist, and I will not pretend to. Questioning the things which I do not understand, and may never come to fully
understand, carries with it a subtle pain. I know that I am not alone in this.
I wish I had all the answers, but no one ever really does. If you are looking
for a satisfactory answer, there is none. I'm afraid that there is no solace to be
found here. Forgive me, I have nothing but the words of Seneca to gift you.
"Death is all that was before us." "What does it matter, after all," he explains,
"whether you cease to be or never begin, when the result of either is that you
do not exist?" Is it really that *simple,* Shira? And even if it wasn't, how would
we ever know? We cannot ever know. Maybe we should stop trying to know.
Can I, or you, or anyone, truly grasp what it is like to exist only in memories,
or be a figure confined within the dimensions of a dream? We are living and
breathing things. Why should I be castigated for being ignorant on the topic
of death, when life is all that I have ever known? If death is all that was before
us, I am convinced that life is all of which contains us. There is a strange and
eternal beauty to be found in that. Don't you think so, too?

Sincerely,

Ifeoma

---

*Ifeoma Okwuka is a current high school senior residing in the Bronx. She has
a genuine love for STEM-related topics and greatly enjoys writing short stories
and personal essays during her spare time.*

## Tell Your Story

## A Prompt from Ifeoma Okwuka

Think back to a time when you grappled with a question to which there were no satisfactory answers. Focus on the emotions or thoughts that emerged from the moment, and explore these emotions/thoughts through any medium of your choice.

# vii

## BY JENNIFER LEE, 2014

*CW: sexual violence, mentions of suicide*

### i. we send beetles to heaven

We meet when I am 7; you are 17.

You lead me to the bathroom with your beetles and white candles; I follow. You lock the door behind me and rummage in the drawers for scissors and tweezers (*shh; it's all safe*). You trisect the beetles and hold them over the flame so they shrivel like raisins but crackle like leaves and fall like ashes to the tiled floor.

I drown in the smoke of crushed legs and heads and hearts—do beetles have hearts?—but then you kiss my ear and warn me not to scream (I didn't know boys and girls are different).

### ii. our bodies press close and you tell me not to tell

Afterwards, my father is too drunk to notice that my eyes are red and my fingers quivering, or that I am limping beneath the sweat-stained air. When we go home, I scrub myself until the blood and tears are gone, and the water icy-cold. I shiver, teeth chattering, until my mother tells me to get out because she needs the shower.

That's when it starts—the wrongness inside me. I scratch at my arms, my wrists, my legs; beetles are gnawing at me, trying to find *outoutout* so I let them bleed out with my blood.

I know their larvae still fester within me, but at least I'm a little bit cleaner.

### iii. i purge myself

My bones go hollow, the beetles are dying, and I cough up acid and crushed wings.

I am 14, and my skin is pink from scrubbing as walls close in around me. Sometimes I think I see you in the hallways or around corners, and I stop walking, only to shiver under cold water until somebody says it's their turn to shower.

I want to go to heaven, but there is no heaven for murderers.

### iv. there is nothing for murderers

I am 15, and a boy kisses me. He is 15, too.

My hands shiver; I cannot breathe. I know I'm dying, but I don't want to go to hell. He tells me to relax (*it's just me*), and I remember (*shh; it's all safe*). I know there is no easy death for killers, so I shake my head as pupae ooze from my pores. I push him away and run, afraid my beetles will devour him, too.

When my math teacher asks to talk to me after class, I freeze. All I can think is that I have an "A"; what does he want,

what does he want,

what does he want?

until I am trembling again, realizing that it's just the two of us together in the room. He says "Sit," but I can't sit; I can feel you in my veins, boiling, snapping, and condemning, until the whole world is consumed by black abdomens and thoraces and elytra until I am on the ground with him kneeling beside me, asking me if I am okay. My nails scrape my arms, saying, *No, don't touch me; nobody touches me but you.* I can feel them (you) hollowing me. I need to get you out, and I cannot obey the command of Stop, Stop, Stop before my teacher leaves to get the nurse.

When he leaves, I can breathe. When I return to class a week later, he says nothing.

### v. the dead have no place in the world of the living; the dead do not speak

The shrink pulls me from class to talk (spider fingers, wasp eyes). She asks how I am, and I say "Fine." She asks me about what happened, and I don't tell her about the beetles.

When she asks me how often I eat, I lick my lips and tell her I eat too much. She blinks, saying "You're Too Skinny," and I tell her that I know. I know I'm skinny; I know I'm breaking, but I cannot feed your beetles; I cannot feed your love.

She asks me if I want to be thinner, prettier, and I say "No:" I know I'm ugly; I know I'm just a husk; I want to fall like ashes; I want to feel your love.

### vi. i miss your love

You are the only one who loved me.

I am 17; you are 27. I don't know where you are, but I live with your beetles and they are my blood (or a symbol of your love).

My mother is dead; your mother was dead, and my father is my father is my father (not all men are created; not all men are created equal). I light a candle and my fingertips graze the flame; the beetles shrivel like raisins but crackle like leaves and fall like ashes to the tiled floor. I am the millions of beetles that live within me. I want to rise like smoke, but killers don't go to heaven. Now I know: I have sent so many beetles to heaven—just kill them, just kill them, just kill them.

***vii. i will send myself to heaven.***

*Jennifer Lee (she/they) grew up in Queens and earned her BA from Columbia University.*

# Khepri

## BY SOPHIA TORRES, 2023

*Jennifer's piece "vii" is a beautiful but dark exploration of a traumatic experience. It was a challenge to respond to, but I hoped to use the same emotionally-affecting language to offer another perspective.*

She believes I'm a parasite. A reminder of the love she's deprived of. She yells *GETOUTOUTOUT* but I am perfectly content where I rest. She theorizes while she lies awake at night. Her heart beats faster, faster, faster, and her nails peel layers of her skin off, hoping to force me out.

Excavate. Expel.

Her skin becomes red and breath slows. Can she understand I cannot leave her? All she does is imagine I crawl through her veins, populate her body, control her as my host. I am the source of her suffering; it never ends (*repulsive*); but (*you do*) I do.

We exist. I exist because she does. We are bound.

Hint: Our anatomies are incompatible but I live because she does.

She always thinks of him—my larvae were dormant and he was not my origin—he is all she thinks of.

When he infects her thoughts,

        the light from yellow wax candles,

    the mutilated beetle,

        the glimmer of light on the scissor he dissected me with.

The memory stalks her so she deteriorates, decomposes. He wants this, and she does not want to see it. The white bathroom she seeks protection in is not a safe space (*he said shh*) but still it offers you some . . . consolation.

The porcelain tub she sits in, *cold,* guards her. Here she lets me bleed, pushes me away, "cleanses" herself but I refuse. She pulls her knees close to her, *cold,* and wraps her frail arms around them. Her thinning hair grazes her bony shoulders as she rocks (*back and forth, back and forth*), scratch, scratch, scratch (*get out*). I cannot leave her; he will not leave her and I try to explain but she will not listen.

No one told her it should not have happened. He is the parasite—grotesque, breaking down her mind, body, compromising her immune system. He wants her immobilized; her life he will not have.

Fact: He is not the warmth of the sun. She is.

She is a nucleus. The center of our universe, my universe.

I am not him.

Our eyes are shaped by a kaleidoscope, but your vision is restricted. I can see you're iridescent.

---

*Sophia Torres (she/her) is a recent graduate and coffee-addict with a degree in political science and English. She is a native New Yorker.*

## Tell Your Story

### A Prompt from Sophia Torres

Write about a moment you overcame a fear or anxiety
that wouldn't go away. How did you feel?
What did you do to overcome it?

# Transformative Love

## BY SARAH RAMIREZ, 2017

*Throughout the course of my life, I have always seen love as something more than just romantic. This piece uncovers how I interpret love and its ability to create change.*

Love is powerful. If you want to change something, the most effective way to go about it is with love. Love is universal in its ability to push past superficiality. It is not formulaic or structured; it is not written on a piece of paper and decided on over a handshake; it is not something that only those in power are able to use. Love is free of form and intangible—beyond limits and beyond definition. A word that is used incessantly can often lose its power; however, when experienced, love has the power to be transformative.

Growing up in church has taught me that without love, all that I do is meaningless. However, not everyone grows up in church, and many do not see love as necessary. In fact, many have become hardened by life's disappointments and obstacles, so they don't recognize love as something that is as important as life, something that is important *to* life. But it is. I say this urgently, because today's news demonstrates the necessity of love without limits. Subway platforms in New York City are riddled with angry voices and loud disputes. I believe that love is gentle enough to heal aches and console cries, but also mighty enough to combat injustice and oppression.

Love, according to Congressman John Lewis, is "a way of being"—meaning that whatever you do, you do with love. Love is the ability to recognize someone else's humanity—and resistance to anything that would degrade or diminish that humanity.

Love does not mean staying silent when you see injustice around you. In fact, it is the exact opposite. Love is correcting and fighting injustice, because injustice is a clear violation of love. We cannot say we "love" when we witness wrongdoing and choose to stay silent. Many people equate love with avoiding conflict, so they stay away from speaking out against it. However, you *can* show love by boldly condemning injustice; you *can* be outraged and still love at the same time. This is called "righteous anger." The anger is what motivates you to want to put an end to the injustice, but the love sustains you and keeps you going. If hate is your sole motive, it makes the quest for justice poisonous and burdensome. In the words of Martin Luther King Jr., "Hate is too great a burden to bear."

"Love your neighbor as yourself" is a well-known Christian commandment. There is no fine print to go along with that verse; there are no conditions. It does not say, "Love your neighbor as yourself, but *only* if they look like you, *only* if they are the same religion as you, *only* if they do good to you, and *only* when it's convenient for you." Our neighbors are not just people who we *want* to help, or who are *easy* to help. Our neighbors are refugees, people of different faiths, skin color, and social status. We cannot sit still as we see groups of people being marginalized. Doing so makes us complicit in their mistreatment.

Yet Christians are called to love not only the victims of injustice, but also the perpetrators. We are to love our enemies, which is easier said than done. *How do you show love to people who don't know what it is? Who seem to be working so vehemently against it?* You love them because they are human. You see them as individuals, and you seek out the goodness in them, that "spark of divine," as John Lewis says, trusting that it's there. You try to understand what happened over the course of their lives that made them this way—angry, vengeful, cold. In a way, loving your enemies is revolutionary; it's righteous, it's radical. "That you beat me, you arrest me, you take me to jail, you almost kill me, but in spite of that, I'm gonna still love you," as Lewis says. Your enemies do not have to have a foothold on your consciousness. You can deny them the power and satisfaction of controlling how you feel, and how you act towards them. In the end, when all is said and done, love will win.

Love is something every human, no matter how hard and cold a heart, responds to. It digs down deep to the core and has the power to shift one's foundation. Love inspires people to rise out of the depths of neutrality. It urges people to speak out against injustice. It is universally understood and craved. It transcends language barriers and time zones. It is a common thread running through people of every nation, so it only makes sense to use love as a catalyst for change.

---

*Sarah Ramirez is a Girls Write Now alumni, class of 2018, and a lover of words and their connecting power. She is pursuing a master's degree in Speech-Language Pathology and looks forward to helping people succeed in communication.*

# What is Love?

## BY NISHAT RAIHANA, 2022

*This piece is a fictional story of a girl who finds beauty in what was initially a place unfamiliar to and uncomfortable for her.*

Reading romance novels into the dead of night until the sun rises and shines brightly upon my sleep-deprived eyes has taught me quite a bit about love. It has taught me that love can feel like I am dancing on top of clouds, the cool breeze softly kissing my cheek. But then, love can also feel like jagged rocks hurled at my heart, cold and piercing to the delicate soul. Love can be heavy as if I am carrying the weight of the world on my shoulders, while Atlas dusts off his hands and leaves me his duties for the rest of the millennium. Still, I think the most important lesson I've learned about love is that it holds no singular form.

As a child, I've often thought about one question: Do my parents love me? When my dad comes home from a long and tiring shift at the hospital but never seems to forget to bring back home a candy treat for his kids, is that love? To my dad, love means putting a smile on his kids' faces and watching as they munch on a candy bar before going to bed. But to him, love also means expecting the best. The day before my little sister's high school placement exam, she had tearfully asked me a heartbreaking question: Will dad still love me if I don't do well on the exam? I tried consoling her, but deep down, we both knew the real answer.

My dad has always had high expectations for us, but that is only because he truly wants the best for us. He wants to see his kids succeed academically because it means a greater potential for a brighter future for each of them. As an immigrant who has struggled his entire life to grasp onto bits and pieces of stability, the only thing he could ever want for his kids is to see them grow up into individuals who do not need to ever worry about when their next meal is going to be, or how they could ever possibly pay for the bills given their financial circumstances. And to my dad, the first step in achieving these hopes is making sure we do well in school, as it will lead to better opportunities down the road. Thus, although my dad's love may not be unconditional, it is without a doubt that he genuinely, transformatively, gave his all to love his three daughters.

The love my best friend and I have for each other is noticeably different from the love my dad offers; however, our love is much like loving a human: a being with countless imperfections and insecurities. My best friend knows every single part of me, from my dreams and ambitions to my deepest, darkest mistakes. And yet, they adamantly continue to support me. Whenever I am with my best friend, the world seems immeasurably brighter. Boisterous laughter and quiet calmness fill our time together until we are left with the realization that our moments will never truly come to an end, because we still have the rest of our lives to spend with each other. And that makes life so much more worth living for.

Despite the intensity of love one can have for their friends and family, I believe that the love we have for ourselves is perhaps the most important love there is. Throughout my life, I have struggled with self-love, just as many others have as well. Much of my teenage years have been spent worrying about what others think of me. From my body weight to my culture and ethnicity, to even my facial features, my opinion of myself depended on what I believed was others' opinions of me. Eventually, I realized my mistakes. When I look at myself in the mirror, I speak to the little girl that I once was, telling her that she is completely perfect the way she is. And although my journey of self-love is still a work in progress, it is undeniable that I've come a long way in making sure that I am able to appreciate the most authentic version of myself.

While growing up, I've often felt the need to build up the walls that surround me, making sure that those who are around me cannot possibly hurt me. Loving others requires being vulnerable, and I believed I loved myself enough that I didn't need love from others. Sooner or later, some of my now closest friends have slipped through the cracks of my wall, teaching me that love transcends even the toughest of barriers. And now, I learned what it really means to love myself: realizing that those who surround me only push me towards growth and towards working on myself every single day. Ultimately, familial love, love between friends, and self-love are all undoubtedly important because it has led to transformative change in not just my life but the lives of many others as well.

*Nishat Raihana is a college freshman currently attending CUNY Hunter College. Some of her interests include gardening and playing video games with her friends. She hopes to study medicine one day and become a physician.*

## Tell Your Story

### A Prompt from Nishat Raihana

Write a list poem exploring the things
that you most love about yourself.

# WRITING
# AND
# PUBLISHING
# TIPS

# WRITING TIPS

*I'm inspired by the work of lots of writers and artists. How can I translate that inspiration into my own creations?*

"Read. Read. Read. Then incorporate the voices and styles you like most into your own writing style. We all "borrow," from other writers without abandoning our own voice—which is the most precious part of any writer's gift."

— JANIS KEARNEY, Girls Write Now Teaching Artist, author of *Only On Sundays: Mahalia Jackson's Long Journey*, and President and Founder of Writing our World Publishing

"Consider the specific elements you love about your favorite writer's work. For example, if you love the way one uses language, and the way another paces their plot, and the way another sets scenes, focus less on exactly how they do it and concentrate on the fact that you appreciate work that uses language, pacing, and scenes in a specific way. Then, try your hand at amplifying those storytelling elements you admire in your own style."

— NANA BREW-HAMMOND, Girls Write Now Mentor Alum, editor of *Relations: An Anthology of African and Diaspora Voices* and author of *Powder Necklace*

"Surround yourself with things you love and things that inspire you: re-read authors you love, listen to music that moves you, hang up art that changes the way you see the world. Ask yourself why you love it and what elements from it you want to incorporate into your own work."

— REBECCA LOWRY WARCHUT, Girls Write Now Mentor and author of *Catastrophe Theory*

*Everyone says writers should "Show, don't tell," but how do I do that? How can I show an aspect of my character or story without just telling the reader about it?*

"Think about the real people you know, they don't go around narrating their life stories to you. You might get some details because they tell you, or because you experienced those events together, but mostly, you learn about them via two things: their words and their actions. With writing, you can do a little reverse engineering: while in real life you'd observe someone's words and actions and make conclusions about what kind of person they are, in writing you can do the opposite, working backwards and putting various pressures on your characters to make them speak or act in a certain way. You can play with how much the reader learns, and when, they don't need to know every single thing about a character on page one, and it's actually more pleasurable to have a character unspool over time."

— ELIZABETH MINKEL, Girls Write Now Mentor, writer, editor, and
co-host of the *Fansplaining* podcast

"Have them talk to other characters. Have them talk to themselves! Put them into scenes where they have to get out of a situation or interact with the world they're in. It'll reveal far more about who they are as a character than if you just tell us what they look like. Don't impose upon them; let them breathe on the page. Trust your readers to understand your intent!"

— RACHEL PRATER, Girls Write Now Mentor, writer, and editor

"Think of yourself as a fly on the wall in the life of your character or the universe of your story. What do you see? What do you hear? How does it make you feel? Reveal your answers to these questions via dialogue, actions, reactions, and interactions to, in turn, unveil the characters and their world to the reader."

— NANA BREW-HAMMOND, Girls Write Now Mentor Alum,
editor of *Relations: An Anthology of African and Diaspora Voices* and
author of *Powder Necklace*

### How can I write realistic-sounding dialogue?

"Listen, listen, listen. Not just to the way people talk in your everyday life, but also the rhythms of dialogue in television, films, and plays. You can learn a lot by reading dialogue, but you learn so much more hearing it, and listening for the choices writers have made. There's no filler in dialogue written for actors, every line belongs in the scene for a specific reason. If you're creating dialogue for a short story or novel, thinking about what would be "voiced" in a scene can help you decide what belongs in dialogue, and what belongs in internal narration."

— ELIZABETH MINKEL, Girls Write Now Mentor, writer, editor, and
co-host of the *Fansplaining* podcast

"The most helpful practice I've found for writing dialogue is listening to conversations around the city—whether in a coffee shop, on the subway, or around my own friends. You'll notice that people rarely speak linearly, or answer each other fully; sometimes each person seems to be having a different conversation. Having your dialogue reflect that can really add depth; not every character will answer a question directly, and people often misunderstand one another. Someone once told me, dialogue is not to convey what the character is saying, but *how* they're saying it."

— MEREDITH WESTGATE, Girls Write Now Mentor and author of
*The Shimmering State*

"Have someone read it aloud, or record yourself reading it. When you play it back to yourself, does it sound natural? If not, tinker with it until it does! People rarely speak in beautiful, complete, perfectly structured sentences."

— REBECCA LOWRY WARCHUT, Girls Write Now Mentor and
author of *Catastrophe Theory*

*Visit www.girlswritenow.org/resources for more*

# PROFESSIONAL WRITING TIPS

### How can I find an agent for my work?

"You can check the Literary Marketplace. Also, look in the acknowledgements of books that you like and are similar to what you write. Often, writers will thank their agent."

— DONNA HILL, Girls Write Now Mentor Alum and author of
*After the Lights Go Down* and *Confessions in B-Flat*

"Not every writer or project needs an agent, so first learn about what an agent offers you (and doesn't) and think about what kinds of publishers you want to work with. Smaller independent publishers and university presses frequently accept un-agented submissions. When you're meeting with potential agents, ask a ton of questions. Your agent is your advocate and advisor, and should be knowledgeable about all sorts of publishing-related matters. Don't feel shy and always feel empowered to ask direct questions about how the agent operates, including the financial elements of the agreement you might enter into."

— MARISA SIEGEL, Girls Write Now Mentor and
author of *Fixed Stars*

There is a subscription fee for Literary Marketplace—If you're in college, see if your library has a subscription. Do an internet search for literary agencies. Go to an agency's website and determine which agents represent books similar in genre to what you're writing. Repeat for each agency.

# WHAT DO AGENTS LOOK FOR IN A QUERY OR BOOK PROPOSAL?

*From Samantha Wekstein of Thompson Literary Agency*
*for a Girls Write Now workshop.*

There are three main components to a query letter:

1. *Introductory Paragraph*
2. *Plot Summary*
3. *Author Bio*

## 1. Introductory Paragraph

- *Title, Word Count, Genre*
- *Why you are sending the project to that agent*
- *Your hook sentence*
- *Any relevant comparative titles\**
- *What you think is wonderful about your book—this is where you can use some fun adjectives—thrilling, poignant, heartfelt, swoony, etc. (sometimes this is covered in the hook).*

## 2. Plot Summary

- *Introduce your character and their world.*
- *Let us know what your character wants—what are their goals, hopes, dreams, etc.. Introduce the obstacles that will prevent your character from getting what they want.*
- *Describe how your character intends to overcome these obstacles.*
- *Describe what your character stands to lose if they don't succeed in overcoming the obstacles—this last one is called "stakes" and it introduces tension into your story and your letter.*
- *For nonfiction, a plot summary is still necessary, but your project may or may not follow a traditional fiction arc. So if it's an essay collection, summarize the themes and give us specific examples of 2-3 stories (this is the same for fictional short story collections). For a memoir or proposal, you can still "summarize your plot" by letting us know in 2-3 paragraphs what your project is about.*

## 3. Bio

*Don't stress about your bio, this is just so agents can get to know you.*

- *Any writing credentials. Do you attend conferences, have you had articles or short stories published? Are you part of any writing groups? These are absolutely not essential.*

- *Where you live, what you do for a living, any hobbies, interests, pets, etc.*
- *Any blogging, social media, publicity connections, follower count, etc.*
- *For nonfiction, your bio is more important because it will communicate your platform. Platform is either your level of fame or expertise. So if you are an expert in a field and have been published—that's something to put in your bio, alternatively if you have 100,000 Twitter followers, that can go in there too. Essentially you want to communicate why you are the best person to be writing this project.*

## *How To Use Comparative Titles

*Not all agents require comp titles (I don't!), but they can be useful to us.*
- *A comp can be used to show us where your project would sit on a bookshelf—for example* Cruel Prince *is perfect for fans of* A Court of Thorns and Roses *and* King of Scars.
- *Alternatively comps can be used to express the flavor of something. For example,* Cruel Prince *has the court politics and intrigue of* The Winner's Kiss *crossed with the seductive and dangerous magic of* A Court of Mist and Fury.
- *You should make sure if you are using comps to have at least one comp title in your genre.*
- *You can also use TV, movies, plays, etc. as comps.*
- *At least one comp should be from the last 5 years.*

## Fiction vs. Nonfiction

- *For fiction, agents will expect you to have a full manuscript prepared and polished. Most agents will request 10–50 pages be included with your original query. Make sure to follow each specific agent's guidelines for what they'd like included in your query package.*

## Book Proposal

- *For most nonfiction (except memoir, which follows the rules of fiction), you will need to have a book proposal prepared. Most book proposals are 40–50 pages. They include several sections—Overview, About the Author, Marketing and Publicity, Specifications, Chapter Summaries, and a writing sample. Once you are under contract, then you will have a certain timeline in which to complete the full book.*
                    —SAMANTHA WEKSTEIN, Thompson Literary Agency

# SELF-REFLECTION PROMPTS:

*What does it feel like to read stories from perspectives that differ from your own? How can learning about someone else's experience change the way you see the world?*

*What themes or ideas do you feel have been relevant for creatives for the past twenty-five years? What themes or ideas do you feel will be relevant for creatives for the next twenty-five years?*

*What is culture? Outside of race and religion, how do you define culture? If someone was writing a scene about someone from your culture, what would you want them to know? Think about writing for readers who are on the margins and in the center of that culture.*

# INCANTATION

# Where Do We Go From Here?
## BY GIFTBELLE LOMOTEY, 2023

*So long as we write, our story goes on.*

Where do we go when darkness and fear spreads, followed by our tears?

Where do we go from here when our loved ones are out of reach?

And we are confronted by our fears

No matter how many times we call them on Facetime

It does not bring them any closer. Where do we go from here?

Where do we go from here when we cannot close the chapter

      on a four-year journey,

Full of many twists, turns, and ups and downs?

Where do we go from here when we cannot experience our last laughs,

Feel the warm embrace of a hug and shed our last tears in person?

As helpful as video chat may be, it doesn't fill the void of not

      having human touch.

Touch is a universal human sense that no technological advancement

      can ever replace.

But as you sit in the confinement of your home, I hope you grow

      more appreciation for it.

As you sit in the confinement of your home, I hope you love yourself deeper.

And as you sit in the confinement of your home, I hope peace,

      love and happiness are keeping you company.

I know being home for most of us is the last place we would like to be.

But to get through these tough times,

We have to be grateful for what we have and not give too much

      energy for what we've lost.

We still have life itself

And the chance to make it better.

---

*Giftbelle Lomotey grew up in the Bronx and is currently continuing to build her skills as a creative.*

## Tell Your Story

### A Prompt from Giftbelle Lomotey

Writers have long used our pens to write, reflect, and re-envision the world around us. It's been said before that the pen is mightier than the sword; it is our greatest tool for change.

As you think about where we go from here, think of your pen. Imagine you have been tasked with writing a new world into existence. What world will you create with ink and paper? Where will your pen lead you to now?

# ABOUT
# GIRLS WRITE NOW

We are a powerhouse of voices that have been ignored or silenced for too long. We are a pipeline into schools and industries in need of new talent and different perspectives. As a community, we follow our hearts, and—through bold, authentic storytelling—inspire people to open theirs. We are Girls Write Now.

For a quarter century, Girls Write Now has been amplifying transformative stories that break down the barriers of gender, race, age, and poverty to mentor and train the next generation of leaders. In addition to being the first writing and mentoring organization of its kind, the nationally award-winning nonprofit has one of the top-ranking programs for social-emotional growth in young people.

Girls Write Now is a creative incubator of female and gender-expansive writers from more than thirty states across the nation who are shaping culture, impacting businesses, and creating change.

This book is a celebration and a dedication to the twenty-five years of mentors, mentees, staff, board, teaching artists, volunteers, and supporters who have defined the organization each step of the way. These creatives, critical thinkers, and game changers have drafted the blueprint for this generation of writers to not just tell their stories, but to decide how those stories are told.

This book is also an invocation for you to be in communion with our authors, past and present, as you discover, or rediscover, the power of your own voice. Our profound thanks to Judith Curr and HarperOne for aligning with our mission to ensure these voices are heard.

—MAYA NUSSBAUM,
Girls Write Now Founder & Executive Director

# 2023 GIRLS WRITE NOW STAFF

Julia Andresakis, *Marketing & Web Design Coordinator*
Azia Armstead, *Fellow*
Marian Caballo, *Editorial Intern & Mentee Alum*
Chelle Carter-Wilson, *Creative Marketing Director,-*
Renisha Conner, *Editorial Intern*
Kathryn Destin, *Special Projects Coordinator*
Morayo Faleyimu, *Senior Editor-in-Residence*
Sally Familia, *Community Coordinator*
Monique Sterling, *Graphic Designer*
Spencer George, *Senior Marketing & Development Coordinator*
Irene Hao, *Editorial Intern & Mentee Alum*
Margery Hannah, *Community Manager, Writing Works*
Dolores Haze, *Editorial Intern*
Ellen Rae Huang, *Development Director*
Jessica Jagtiani, *Community Manager, Writing 360*
Mi So Jeong, *Operations Manager*
Vahni Kurra, *Senior Community & Marketing Coordinator*
Kelsey LePage, *Development Manager*
Molly MacDermot, *Director of Special Initiatives*
Emily Mendelson, *Community Manager, Publishing 360*
Emily Méndez, *Editor-In-Residence*
Elmer Meza, *Salesforce & Systems Manager*
Maya Nussbaum, *Founder & Executive Director*
Daniella Olibrice, *Director, People & Culture*
Emily Oppenheimer, *Senior Grants Manager*
Lisbett Rodriguez, *Senior Programs & Systems Coordinator*
Jeanine Marie Russaw, *Community Coordinator*
Erica Silberman, *Director of Curriculum & Engagement*
Karen van de Vrande, *Development Consultant*
Zuzanna Wasiluk, *Editorial Intern & Mentee Alum*
Joe Wilson, *Director of Information Technology*

We are grateful to the countless institutions and individuals who have supported our work through their generous contributions. Visit our website at girlswritenow.org to view the extended list.